Spirituality at Work

Spirituality at work

10 Ways to Balance Your Life on the Job

Gregory F. A. Pierce

LOYOLAPRESS.

CHICAGO

LOYOLAPRESS.
3441 N. ASHLAND AVENUE
CHICAGO, ILLINOIS 60657
(800) 621-1008
WWW.LOYOLABOOKS.ORG

All of the quotes used as sidebars and some of the other quotes used throughout this book originally came from individuals who participated in an informal e-mail group called "Faith and Work in Cyberspace" and are attributed and used with permission. The quote from David Whyte in the conclusion is used with permission of Many Rivers Company, P.O. Box 868, Langley, Washington 98260. All other quotations were considered fair use. Sources are listed at the end of the book.

Cover and interior design by Erin VanWerden

Library of Congress Cataloging-in-Publication Data
Pierce, Gregory F.
 Spirituality at work : 10 ways to balance your life on the job / Gregory F.A. Pierce.
  p. cm.
 ISBN 0-8294-2116-5
 1. Employees—Religious life. 2. Work—Religious aspects—Christianity. I. Title.
BV4593.P54 2005
248.8'8—dc22

                                                                    2004021340

Printed in the United States of America
05 06 07 08 09 10 11 Bang 10 9 8 7 6 5 4 3 2 1

Dedication of the Paperback Edition

To Russ Barta and Ed Marciniak

Brothers-in-law founders of the National Center for the Laity,
who passionately proclaimed the vocation of the laity in
and to the world. Thanks for all your good work.
May you both rest in well-deserved peace.

The Mount of Horeb

Elijah was told, "Go out and stand on the mountain before Yahweh." For at that moment Yahweh was going by. A mighty hurricane split the mountains and shattered the rocks before Yahweh. But Yahweh was not in the hurricane. And after the hurricane, an earthquake. But Yahweh was not in the earthquake. And after the earthquake, fire. But Yahweh was not in the fire. And after the fire, a light murmuring sound. And when Elijah heard this, he covered his face with his cloak.

1 Kings 19:11–13 (NJB)

I was looking for God.

*And so I left behind
my family,
my job,
my community
and set out.*

*First I went to a church,
but I did not find God in the church.*

*Next I retreated to a monastery,
but I did not meet God in the monastery.*

*Then I made a pilgrimage to the holy sites,
but I did not discover God in the holy sites.*

*Discouraged,
I returned home.*

*As I hugged my family,
I felt the presence of God.*

*When I resumed my job,
I perceived God's hand guiding my work.*

*In the midst of involvement in my community,
I realized that God was there with me.*

*In awe,
I hid my face in my cloak.*

Gregory F. Augustine Pierce

Contents

Preface

When *Spirituality at Work* was first published in hardcover in 2001, the very idea of trying to find God in the midst of the hustle and bustle of daily life—and especially in a workplace that is being experienced as devoid of the holy, the sacred, the transcendent, the ultimately meaningful—seemed new and perhaps a bit odd, if not downright silly, to many people. But since then, the entire spirituality of work "movement" has burst upon the scene in no uncertain terms. A variety of good books have since been published on the subject, and even *Fortune* magazine ran a cover story subtitled "The Surprising Quest for Spiritual Renewal in the American Workplace."

The positive reaction I have received to my book has convinced me that people are hungry for ways to balance their work lives with their personal, family, community, and church responsibilities. I have spoken with groups from all over the United States—from San Diego to Scranton, from Memphis to Cincinnati, from North Carolina to Spokane—and my e-mail list now has over 1,000 participants, all of whom are struggling (as I am) to figure out how we can really practice "spirituality at work."

What I have learned from those with whom I have talked is that the spirituality of work is an authentic spirituality, not a second-class cousin to the real thing. There are many people who regularly experience God in their work, and the awareness of this presence transforms how they do their work. If these people were in the majority in most workplaces, this would be a very different world indeed.

I am now even more convinced that for any spirituality (including the spirituality of work) to be authentic, it must change the way we act. I see a lot of what is called "spirituality of work" or "marketplace ministry" being used as the latest management technique to make workers more productive or help them feel better about their jobs. The key to the spirituality of work, however, is that when we finally recognize that we are in the presence of God—whatever word or words we use for that presence—we simply cannot continue to operate in the same way we would if we were not in that presence. Ipso facto, as we used to say in my high school Latin class, we humans automatically act much differently when we are in touch with the true God—the Real One, the Ultimate Big Unit, the Original Sine Qua Non. We can't help ourselves. If we don't act any differently when we are aware of the divine presence than we do when we are oblivious to that presence, we've probably got the wrong god in the first place.

As Jesus might have put it, by our fruits we will know whether or not we are practicing an authentic and helpful spirituality. So let's not fool ourselves. We cannot practice a spirituality of work unless we are willing to be better—more honest, creative, compassionate, competent—workers, no matter what profession or occupation or vocation we find ourselves in, and any spirituality that merely makes us feel good is bogus.

Finally, I would like to reemphasize that the spirituality of work is for everyone, not just managers or professionals or white-collar workers. I am nervous about all the books being written for CEOs and top managers in business; as if they are the only or most important ones who need to find God in their work. If the spirituality of work does not work for the secretary, the farmer, the police officer, the machinist, the sanitation worker, the grocer, the tailor, and the tollbooth operator, then it is not a fully matured spirituality.

If you'd like to join this ongoing conversation, just send me an e-mail at spiritualitywork@aol.com.

Thank you for all your good work.

Gregory F. Augustine Pierce
Chicago, Illinois

Introduction

A Spirituality for the Piety Impaired

"Bidden or not bidden, God is present." These words, carved in Latin over the door to the office of philosopher and psychoanalyst Carl Jung, are as true or false in the workplace as they are anywhere else. If we don't believe them—really, functionally, in our gut—then the idea that work can be a source of spiritual insight, comfort, challenge, and growth is absurd and a folly. If we do believe them, then the workplace becomes just one more place, one more opportunity, where the divine reality can be encountered in a tangible way.

Why would we want to look for God in our work? The simplest answer is that most of us spend so much of our time working that it would be a shame if we couldn't find God there. A more complex reason is that there is a creative energy in work that is somehow tied to God's creative energy. If we can understand and enter into that connection, perhaps we can use it to transform the workplace into something quite remarkable. While I believe the spirituality of work has its roots in the best parts of at least the Christian tradition (I don't feel qualified to discuss how this spirituality fits with other faiths), I also believe that the spirituality of work is different from—and in some ways antithetical to—the prevailing Christian spirituality, which I would call "contemplative" or even "monastic."

You will not find here a pious approach to the spirituality of work. I like to joke that I consider myself "piety impaired," but I also admit that I am not comfortable with displays of religiousity, especially in the workplace. I do not think that the spirituality of work is about organizing prayer groups or Bible study programs in the office, factory, or farmhouse. If people want to do that, it is fine with me—but don't ask me to join. Nor am I terribly eager to discuss my religious beliefs with others in the workplace. If someone wants to ask me about what I believe or why I act a certain way, I am certainly willing to talk with them. But you won't find me walking around the office saying "Thank God" or "Praise the Lord."

The spirituality of work that interests me is one that comes out of the work itself, one that allows us to get in touch with the God who is always present in our workplaces, whether "bidden or not bidden." This kind of spirituality has little to do with piety and much more to do with our becoming aware of the intrinsically spiritual nature of the work we are doing and then acting on that awareness. Authentic spirituality—at least in the Judeo-Christian tradition—is as much about making hard choices in our daily lives, about working with others to make the world a better place, and about loving our neighbor and even our enemy as it is about worship and prayer. For this reason, I believe that the spirituality of work can be explained and described primarily in secular language, a language much more easily understood by the average person, who is often not a religious professional or even particularly devout. This language also has the added advantage of being accessible to those of other faiths and traditions and even to those of no particular religious background or belief.

This book is an exploration of the spirituality of work. It is an attempt to investigate whether and how the reality that we call God can be accessed in the midst of the hustle and bustle of our daily work lives. This is by no means a comprehensive or definitive exercise. I have only been aware of the possibility of getting in tune with the divine presence through my work for the last decade or so, and—as anyone who works with me will attest—I fail in my attempts much more often than I succeed. So I offer these reflections more out of an attempt to begin a dialogue with others than to claim that I have figured out what the spirituality of work is or how it can be practiced.

I have been conducting this dialogue on the Internet for the past few years with more than three hundred people in a group called "Faith and Work in Cyberspace." Every couple of weeks, I have sent out an e-mail on one of the ideas found in this book and have invited the group to send me their thoughts, experiences, and examples. More than anything else, their provocative responses have helped shape my thinking on practicing the disciplines of the spirituality of work. You will find their comments sprinkled throughout this book, and there is an invitation in the conclusion for you to join our ongoing dialogue.

So you see, this is not your typical book on spirituality. It is focused on an area of our lives that is often viewed as inconsequential—if not outright hostile—to our spiritual lives, and it tries to use the language of the workplace rather than the language of religion to talk about spiritual matters. Despite these caveats, I invite you to join me on this search for the God who, bidden or unbidden, is always present in our work.

Gregory F. Augustine Pierce
Chicago, Illinois

Chapter 1

What Does It Mean to Be Spiritual at Work?

Every act leaves the world with a deeper or a fainter impress of God.

Alfred North Whitehead

1

For many people—well, probably for most—*spirituality* means getting away from the busy world in one way or another. We get away to pray, to meditate or reflect, or to worship. If someone suggests that spirituality can be practiced just as well in the midst of our daily lives—on our jobs, with our families, in our community—the very definition of what we mean by *spirituality* is called into question.

Is "Spirituality of Work" an Oxymoron?

It seems that "spirituality of work" is an oxymoron: two ideas that at first do not seem to go together, like "jumbo shrimp" or "tough love."

But what if spirituality really *doesn't* exist (or at least cannot be discovered) in the hustle and bustle of daily life, and especially in the workplace? For Christians at least, this must be a heresy of some sort. Isn't God everywhere? Doesn't the doctrine of the Incarnation mean that the entire material world has been infused with divine life?

And if spirituality cannot be discovered in the primary, ordinary activities of ordinary people, then hasn't spirituality itself been appropriated by a special interest group—the "You must get away from the world to find God" lobby, the "I'm holy and you're not" school of religion? The rest of us—the busy office workers or factory workers or farmworkers; the parents with small children; the hospice volunteers; the local precinct captains or civic leaders—are all relegated to a part-time spirituality that is snatched in the minutes and hours we can get away from our myriad responsibilities. We become amateurs in the spirituality game. And if we are merely standing on the outside of the spiritual life and looking in, no wonder we become envious of the monk on the mountaintop.

Therefore, I am going to assume that spirituality *can* be practiced in our work. I'm going to assume that there is a spirituality of work that can be every bit as rich, satisfying, challenging, and compelling as the most traditional monastic or mystical spirituality.

In the Buddhist tradition there is a story of a woman who finally became enlightened. When she was asked what the difference was, she described it this way: "Before I was enlightened, I chopped wood and I hauled water. After I was enlightened, I chopped wood and I hauled water." I think that the spirituality of work is much like this. We can be doing exactly the same work before we begin practicing the spirituality of work as we do afterward. But both our spirituality and our work are changed by the very act of making the connection.

If, as I assume, there is such a thing as a "spirituality of work," how do we find it? Does this spirituality exist as a serious, long-term, disciplined, spiritual path? Certainly not in the way that some of the more traditional spiritualities do. There are very few good books on the spirituality of work. It is not a spirituality that is preached from the pulpit very often. There are few saints who espoused or practiced spirituality that was based on their work in the world. There are no schools for this spirituality, and few retreat centers specialize in it. There is no international organization or movement, no headquarters, and no bible (unless you count the Bible—but that's another discussion).

Recently, however, spirituality has become the latest fad in corporate culture. The many books, seminars, articles, and gurus now pushing "spirituality" in the workplace should serve as warnings to us. "Spirituality of work" could easily become a soft, individualistic, emotional "fix" used merely to make people feel better about the status quo or work harder for less money.

A true spirituality of work is not about quick fixes. As theologian John Shea says, "People who think they can control spirit are making a fundamental mistake. We do not control the spirit. That spirit challenges us to go places and do things we would otherwise avoid." "Genuine spirituality," as writer Eugene Kennedy has pointed out, "makes demands on us, challenges us to overcome selfishness, to love from the depths of ourselves so that we may establish community with others despite our sinful human condition."

Is Work a Punishment for Our Sins?

For most people, work can seem to be the opposite of spirituality. "If work is so great," said columnist Mike Royko, "why do they have to pay us to do it?" "I never did like to work, and I don't deny it," said

Abraham Lincoln. "I'd rather read, tell stories, crack jokes, talk, laugh—anything but work."

In the late fifties and early sixties, there was a popular television program called *The Many Loves of Dobie Gillis*. One of the characters on the show (played by actor Bob Denver, who went on to become Gilligan of *Gilligan's Island*) was Maynard G. Krebs. Maynard was a beatnik. A few years later he would have been called a hippie. He always wore the same ratty old sweatshirt, never went to class, and whenever anyone would suggest that he get a job, he would scream in a high-pitched tone of utter contempt and terror, "WORK!" That one word, delivered perfectly every time, summed up popular culture's view of work: at best a necessary evil, something we do because we have to, something to be avoided if at all possible, and certainly not the locus of our spiritual lives.

But if you don't have work to do, you are viewed with great suspicion in our society. It is almost as if work defines who we are. Those without "gainful employment"—welfare recipients, stay-at-home parents, even retired people—are often considered less worthy, less productive members of society than those with jobs, no matter how little those jobs contribute to the betterment of society.

> **I feel that monastic spirituality** has forced us to adopt a reflective mode, but I'm most alive when I'm creative, stimulated, and exercising the talents and abilities that God gave me. God comes alive to me personally when I'm active, alive, contributing, and growing.
>
> Personally, I feel that God partially loses opportunities to act through the hands of others when I allow myself to become isolated or attached to the walls that separate me from community. My experience tells me that God acts powerfully through those around me at work, through my family and friends, and through strangers I run into.
>
> **Patrick Brown**—business executive
> Milwaukee, Wisconsin

It is not just secular society that shapes our view of work, however. In many corners of religion, work is often viewed as negative or, at best, is ignored as irrelevant to the search for God.

Let's start with one of the most foundational stories of the Judeo-Christian tradition: the story of the original sin. Adam and Eve are living in the Garden of Eden, perfectly happy and presumably with plenty of time for spiritual pursuits. They tend the garden, but it is pleasant, fulfilling work. From the start, then, work is a spiritually enriching endeavor. Then the pair do something wrong. Whatever it is, the punishment is clear: They are banished from the Garden forever, and from then on their work will be by the sweat of their brow. Thus tending the garden transformed into WORK! (Maynard G. Krebs would understand this story.)

> **Just as quiet,** solitude, withdrawal, and meditation are elements of the spirituality of contemplation, so are hustle, bustle, noise, crowds, and complexity the elements of the spirituality of engagement with the world. We must, I believe, shift our thinking from "How can I be spiritual in spite of these things?" to "What is the methodology of appreciating and living a spirituality in the midst of them?" As long as the ordinary incidents of daily life are seen as separate from, or even opposed to, spirituality, we will be frustrated because we will have defined ourselves as essentially separated from that which we seek.
>
> **Joseph A. Davies**—lawyer, husband, and father, Denver, Colorado

This negative religious attitude toward work is not an isolated example. Many years ago, Harper & Row published a book titled *Christian Spirituality: The Essential Guide to the Most Influential Spiritual Writings of the Christian Tradition.* This is a 690-page, $34.95 hardcover book that promises "Nearly 2000 years of Christian spiritual writing presented, examined, and summarized . . . by more than twenty esteemed professors and religious scholars. . . . A detailed overview of the broad spectrum of Christian history from its inception to the present day."

One of the features of the book is an extensive index. There are citations listed for asceticism, contemplation, meditation, prayer, and so forth. When I checked for those things that I spend 90 percent of

There are jobs that pay poorly, that are difficult, and that are not very rewarding. For many people, work may feel like a necessary evil. Yet I have found that we all want work to be a positive and meaningful experience. We all want to be valued as persons, and work is part of who we are. When we say our work is not spiritual, we devalue a part of who we are. And if we do not value ourselves, then we treat others—employees, coworkers, customers—with contempt. If we see our work as only a necessary evil, we begin to see ourselves the same way. Every bad work experience I have had resulted from people not valuing themselves and others.

We are called to communicate God's love in the world, and we do so through all our actions, including our work. We allow work to lose its sacredness when we devalue it and the people who do it. This then allows us to send people into unsafe jobs and make them do unfulfilling tasks. We—not God—make work meaningless.

Mark Linder—municipal department director, husband, Santa Cruz, California

my waking time on, however, this is what I found: under "work," no listing; "job," no listing; "labor," no listing. I then looked under "community," "politics," and "social justice." Still no listings. I went to "family," sure that I would find something. There was nothing. Finally, under "marriage," I found one citation for two separate entries; it read "marriage, renunciation of." When I looked under "children" and found only "children, as evil," I knew that I would never actually read the book.

It's not that in two thousand years nothing has been written about work or community or family life in the Christian spiritual tradition. But that a major publisher could bring out an important book—one that I am sure found its way into seminary libraries and onto the bookshelves of clergy and of laypeople—that purported to summarize Christian spirituality without mentioning these basic realities of people's lives shows that daily, ordinary work is either ignored or held suspect by much of organized religion.

Are There Disciplines for the Spirituality of Work?

Why is so little good material on the spirituality of work coming out of the Christian tradition?

One reason is simply that practitioners of the contemplative tradition have convinced just about everyone that if we want to align ourselves and our environment with God then we must get away from the world, at least for a time. "Silence, solitude, and simplicity" is the motto of traditional, contemplative spirituality, while "noise, crowds, and complexity" would describe the "spiritual" view of the normal workday.

Another reason that the spirituality of work has not become a familiar and accepted concept is that, unlike many other spiritualities, it has no distinctive set of disciplines that have been developed by those who practice spirituality in the workplace. There are no established practices that people can follow to make such spirituality a reality. If God can be found in the hustle and bustle of daily life, in noisy homes or factories, in crowded subways and full classrooms, in complex business deals or political decisions, how exactly does it happen?

In his influential book *A Celebration of Discipline,* Richard Foster identifies several regular practices that he felt were essential to the spiritual life. He calls them the "classical disciplines" and includes meditation, prayer, fasting, study, simplicity, solitude, submission, service, confession, worship, guidance, and celebration. Certainly Foster would argue that these traditional spiritual disciplines are just what busy people need. "In contemporary society our Adversary majors in three things: noise, hurry, and crowds," he writes. "If we hope to move beyond the superficialities of our culture, including our religious culture, we must be willing to go down into the re-creating silences, into the inner world of contemplation."

There is a problem, however, with trying to adapt the contemplative spiritual disciplines to the workplace: it doesn't seem to work for the great majority of people. I think that it doesn't work precisely because the contemplative disciplines rely on our getting away from the world. Parker Palmer put his finger on this problem in his book *The Active Life:*

> People who try to live by monastic norms sometimes fall so short ("I just can't find an hour a day to meditate") that they end up feeling guilty about leading "unspiritual" lives. People caught in the gap between monastic values and the demands of active life sometimes simply abandon the spiritual quest. And people who follow a spirituality that does not always respect the energies of action are sometimes led into passivity and withdrawal, into a diminishment of their own spirits.
>
> In the spiritual literature of our time, it is not difficult to find the world of action portrayed as an arena of ego and power, while the world of contemplation is pictured as a realm of light and grace. I have often read, for example, that the treasure of "true self" can be found as we draw back from active life and enter into contemplative prayer. Less often have I read that this treasure can be found in our struggles to work, create, and care in the world of action.

Being in a sales position, I have many opportunities to make the wrong decision (b.s., lie, stretch the truth, etc.). I suppose that there are endless opportunities for doing harm to others and ourselves at work by losing touch with the spiritual basis for our decision making. Perhaps one can have no spiritual life at all and still make the right decisions, but all I know is that I need guidance and good examples in my life. My religious upbringing and faith, as well as seeing others put their faith into action in the workplace, helps keep me on track.

Tom Walsh—shopping-center leasing representative, husband, and father
Palatine, Illinois

If a spirituality of work is going to be successful, it cannot be based on practices that take us away from the daily grind. Instead, we must develop practices that allow us to transform that "grind" into "grist" for our spiritual mills. The disciplines of the spirituality of work must arise from and be compatible with our work, rather than attempt to overlay the workplace with practices drawn from another place, time, and life situation.

How Spiritual Was Jesus?

Spirituality is a word that evokes all kinds of warm, fuzzy feelings. We think of sitting on a mountaintop or seashore, watching the sun rise or set while we contemplate the eternal verities of life. Or we remember times of peace and quiet—perhaps on a retreat or day of recollection—when we were able to pray, or read, or meditate for hours. Or we jealously guard the few moments in each day or week when we practice our spirituality. But what, exactly, is spirituality? One wag has said that trying to define spirituality is like trying to nail Jell-O to a tree. Yet spirituality is one of those things for which "we know it when we see it" applies.

The first mistake in trying to define or understand spirituality is to confuse it with religion or piety. We think that because we go to church or pray or meditate or do any of a myriad of religious practices we are being spiritual. Not necessarily. There is a story of an abbot and a young monk who are invited to supper at the home of a family. The family is honored to have these holy guests and go out of their way (and probably way beyond their budget) to put on a magnificent meal. The young monk, however, has taken a vow to fast, and so he declines all but a single stalk of celery, which he carves up nicely and eats. On the way back to the monastery, the abbot says to the young monk, "The next time, fast from your virtue."

The young monk had mistaken the religious practice of fasting for true spirituality. He would have been closer to the mark had he eschewed his fast and entered into the hospitality and generosity of his hosts.

Christians, of course, have the abbot's understanding of spirituality firmly in our tradition, thanks primarily to Jesus himself. While Jesus prayed and fasted and went to synagogue, he always made clear that religious practices were a means to an end, not an end in themselves.

If the Sabbath ban against activity got in the way of the disciples' helping others (or even, in one story, of the disciples' satisfying their hunger), then Jesus told them to drop it. He was always "eating and drinking" with sinners, not insisting that they join him in prayer. He taught his disciples to pray in private and to always put the law of love above the law of Moses. (Notice that when he forgave the woman caught in adultery he did not recommend that she become a nun. He simply told her to sin no more.)

Jesus was not a monk, and he did not recommend that his disciples become monks. In fact, the Christian monastic tradition started centuries after the beginning of the church. Jesus was no doubt aware of the get-away-from-the-world tradition, since it is fairly well established that the Essene community—a group of Jews organized somewhat like today's monastics—was operating at the time of Jesus and that he almost surely would have known about it. Perhaps he visited the Essenes, learned from them, even stayed with them for a time. But he did not become one of them, nor did he encourage his disciples to emulate them.

The spirituality of Jesus was clearly much more oriented to staying in the world than to getting away from it. How have we come to think otherwise?

What Do Monks Have to Do with It?

There's a little book that remains on the list of spiritual best-sellers five hundred years after it was written: *The Imitation of Christ* by Thomas à Kempis. New translations and editions of this book come out every year, proving that many people find relevant what an obscure monk wrote in the late Middle Ages.

Because it is such a classic (and because I thought getting away from the world was what spirituality was all about), I used to read

The Imitation of Christ when I was younger as part of a daily discipline of "spiritual reading." Now, many years later, I go back and reread some of the things that Thomas à Kempis wrote, and I cringe. "This is the highest wisdom, by contempt of the world to tend toward the kingdom of heaven," or "Truly it is misery even to live upon the earth," or, approvingly quoting the Roman poet Seneca, "Every time I walk among men, I come back less a man."

I use poor Brother Kempis as a whipping boy not because I have anything against him. I am merely using his writings as an archetype of what many of us think of when we think about spirituality: that it is ascetic, suspicious of the world, based on monastic lifestyles and disciplines, and pretty much ignorant or even contemptuous of the experience of everyday life—work, family, and civic affairs.

It is true that there are traditions within Christianity that have emphasized a spirituality of daily life that includes work. Thérèse of Lisieux, "the Little Flower," talked about the "little way" of spirituality in her daily life. Ignatius of Loyola, Francis of Assisi, Francis de Sales, Mother Teresa, and many others had a clear sense that God can be found in the ordinary lives of people. Even Benedict, the founder of monasticism himself, taught that work and prayer were both essential to the spiritual life. And

If spirituality deals with our relationship with God, then everyone has something to say about it. Our language, images, and metaphors will vary according to who we are and what our experiences and insights are. We've all heard little children describe their understanding of God and their relationship with the divine mystery. Poets and spiritual writers do the same. But so do ordinary people who see God at work in their lives, who see everything as a continuation of creation and incarnation (to use theological terms). Probably the gift that most of us can give others regarding spirituality is to share, in our own language and images, our experiences of God and our struggles to be faithful.

Maria Leonard—book editor
Chicago, Illinois

Martin Luther, the founder of the Protestant Reformation, had a very complete theology of what he called "the priesthood of all believers" that put people's daily work at the center of their Christian vocations.

On the other hand, in the story of Mary and Martha, Jesus affirmed Mary because she took time away from work to listen to him teach, and he mildly reprimanded Martha for being worried about too many things (at that moment, getting dinner on the table). Jesus said that Mary had chosen "the better part." And that better part has been almost universally understood to mean that leaving the cooking and dishes to someone else and sitting in contemplation at the feet of the Lord is the right choice for those who would follow Jesus.

And who are the Christian saints? For the most part, they are men and women in religious orders who are holy not for what they have done in the world but for what they have done in or for the church. And almost all of them share a strong strain of contemplative spirituality. The Little Flower may have believed in the "little way," but she did so from inside a Carmelite convent from the age of fifteen. And Francis of Assisi may have taught love of the common person, but he sure didn't have much use for his father's textile business. One of the earliest saints, Simeon Stylites, spent most of his religious life praying on a pillar in the desert, not working for a living. Meanwhile, the Vatican has announced that it is looking for a married couple to canonize but is having trouble finding even one set of saintly spouses in two thousand years of Christianity!

It's easy to see why the prevailing spirituality in mainline Christianity is based on the idea of getting away from the world, at least for a time. This type of spirituality is kept alive and promoted by a very strong network of institutions, including monasteries, retreat centers, local parishes, publishing houses, and so forth. We are taught that if we want to find God we have to adopt a more contemplative spirituality. There is a resurgence of interest in monastic life as seen by the popularity of writers such as Thomas Keating, Kathleen Norris, Henri Nouwen, James Behrens, Thomas Moore, and Thomas Merton. In his book *Beyond the Walls: Monastic Wisdom for Everyday*

Life, Paul Wilkes describes the attraction he feels as a layperson for the monastic tradition:

> The desire to live life on some higher plain, with some greater goal—more spiritually, more monastic—would not leave me. It was strange: monasticism had spoken to my life in so many ways, although I had never been a monk. I continually referred to the practices and values of the monastic community as practices and values that made sense in the outside world.

Artist Sr. Mary Southard uses the image of swimming in a deep pool of water. She says that she needs to "dive deep" into the water of contemplation on a regular basis to get away from the distractions of daily life. Only then is she able to function on the "surface" of action.

These are all attractive images to me, as they may well be to you. My life is full of hustle and bustle. I am married and have three school-age children, I run my own book-publishing business, I coach kids at baseball, and I am involved in several neighborhood, civic, and political organizations. My parish is constantly encouraging me to get involved in one or more of its lay ministries. Rather than silence, solitude, and simplicity, my life is one of noise, crowds, and complexity. So the idea of getting away from

There is a proclivity in business to demand "emotional work" from employees rather than setting up conditions in which genuine good feelings can emerge. For example, do I really like the artificial niceness of flight attendants? No, but it does get me through the ride. Likewise, amenities at work can exist for dubious reasons. Do I like the fact that the food is gourmet and nearly free at some high-tech business campuses mainly so that employees will never leave work? No, but some people never feel more alive than when they are working on a super-special project with their team that requires them to stay at work all night.

So, work is often a mess: the gold and the fool's gold are often found side by side.

Thomas Holahan, CSP — Catholic priest, campus minister, and member of a religious community, Boulder, Colorado

Here are my assumptions about spirituality:

1. God exists and we are in relationship with God. Our "work"—both inner and outer work—is to encounter this reality with our whole self.

2. People are spiritual beings. All that we are and do is inherently spiritual. Spirituality is already present in all aspects of our lives, whether it is acknowledged or not.

3. Creativity is God's gift to all people, not just artists. Creativity is the source of everything that refreshes us and gives us life.

4. A healthy ecumenism not only permits but invites us to speak from our own religious traditions while expressing openness to ideas, practices, and principles from other traditions.

Julie Cowie—Baptist minister, business consultant, South Haven, Michigan

the world—at least for a time—is tempting.

But is getting away from the world the only or even the best way to encounter God? If it is, then there's nothing much to talk about. Spirituality is, then, primarily an activity for an elite—that is, for those who are able and willing to practice the traditional contemplative disciplines. For most laypeople—unless we are willing to abandon our families, quit our jobs, and resign from our volunteer activities—our spirituality will be relegated to a very small part of our lives. We might snatch an hour here or there. We might even get away on an annual weekend retreat. We could get up an hour earlier to pray or meditate or sneak off to church. We might spend our lunchtime studying the Bible or communing with God through nature. But in the end, for 90 to 95 percent of our waking time, we will continue to be surrounded by noise, crowds, and complexity, and there's not much—spiritually speaking—that we can do about it.

Contemplative practices may help us cope better with our daily lives. They might make us calmer, more at peace, and more aware of the needs of others and the presence of God. But unless we can learn to find God in the midst of the hustle and bustle of daily life, we will always have that nagging feeling that we should be doing more or finding more time for our spirituality. In a way, we would have every right to be jealous of that monk on a mountaintop who has virtually unlimited time to devote to spiritual pursuits.

I value what those who practice contemplative spirituality provide for the rest of us. By their radical lifestyle they constantly call into question our assumptions about what we value and how we live. Their thoughts and insights into the nature of human and divine life are the bedrock of Christian thought. But I am raising a much more basic question: Is spirituality, by definition, getting away from the world? I'd like to propose that this is but one spiritual strategy, albeit the dominant one. There is another perhaps more difficult and dangerous strategy that involves getting *into* the world rather than away from it. It is a spirituality of noise, crowds, and complexity, a spirituality that can be found right at the surface of the pool, not in its depths; it is a spirituality of work.

What Is the Definition of Spirituality?

If spirituality is not synonymous with getting away from the world, then we had better define what we are talking about. How's this for an attempt to nail Jell-O to a tree:

> **Spirituality is a disciplined attempt to align ourselves and our environment with God and to incarnate (enflesh, make real, materialize) God's spirit in the world.**

Under this definition, there can be all kinds of spirituality—including a spirituality of work—and spirituality does not necessarily equal contemplation.

I think that the best of the contemplative tradition agrees with me. Many of the monks and mystics teach that the essence of spirituality is not about getting away from the world but about getting deeper into it. For example, Brother Lawrence, a seventeenth-century monk, wrote this about spirituality and work in his classic little book, *The Practice of the Presence of God:* "People delude themselves when they think that prayer time ought to be different from the rest of their lives. God asks us to be united with him just as much by our actions when we are busy as by our prayer during our devotions." In fact, Brother Lawrence said that he was more united with God when he was busy with ordinary activities than when he left them for prayer time.

Trappist Fr. James Behrens, in his book *Grace Is Everywhere: Reflections of an Aspiring Monk,* says, "It may be tempting to say that a 'religious' experience like the Mass is a more refined one than sitting on a porch or walking a dog, but I think it is best to say that God finds us where we are." And as Paul Wilkes points out in his book, "Monks seek their Pure Land within the confines of a monastery. For the rest of us, our Pure Land can be our homes, our workplace, our trips to the supermarket, and our sitting in town-council meetings."

If it is possible to find God in the hustle and bustle of daily life, rather than only by getting away from it, then that would—almost by definition—require different spiritual practices from the ones most of us are used to. This book is an attempt to explore that different spirituality.

What Is the Definition of Work?

The definition of work is almost as problematic as the definition of spirituality. *The Oxford English Dictionary* gives the noun work thirty-four different meanings and the verb thirty-nine. Do we mean only paid employment? What about all the volunteer work people do for free? What if someone is involuntarily unemployed or has retired? The economists often want to equate work with paid employment, but most people's experience is that much of their daily work is unpaid, unrecognized, and often performed far away from the "marketplace."

Popular culture presents work as, at best, a tedious distraction and, at worst, a "rat race" in which—in the words of comedian Lily Tomlin—"even if you win, you're still a rat." (If you don't agree, try thinking of ten movies or television shows that portray work in a positive way—then eliminate those that are about teachers, medical personnel, parents, or a very few other service jobs.)

The prevailing view is that some work may be meaningful and fulfilling but most is not. While it is acknowledged that some people may love their work and feel they are helping others, it is thought that these people are few and far between and that most of them are either highly paid white-collar workers or in the helping professions. The perception is that for most people work is alienating, oppressive, exhausting—anything but spiritual.

But I think it is precisely because the workplace is often not spiritual by nature that what work needs more than anything else is an authentic spirituality. So let's try this definition of work:

Work is all the effort (paid or unpaid) we exert to make the world a better place, a little closer to the way God would have things.

Under this definition all work—our jobs; fixing and cleaning up our homes; our church and community involvement; caring for parents, children, relatives, friends, and strangers; even some of our hobbies—can be seen in a spiritual light. Likewise, the toll collector on the expressway or the sanitation worker picking up the garbage has as much opportunity to discover the presence of God in the workplace as the lawyer or the nurse or the businessperson.

Whether we are overpaid, underpaid, unpaid, or correctly paid; whether we enjoy, hate, or tolerate our work; and whether or not our work has obvious social value—these might all be important issues in the spirituality of work, but they do not determine the spiritual value of our work.

What Is the Spirituality of Work?

If you buy my definitions of spirituality and of work, then we can define a spirituality of work.

The spirituality of work is a disciplined attempt to align ourselves and our environment with God and to incarnate God's spirit in the world through all the effort (paid and unpaid) we exert to make the world a better place, a little closer to the way God would have things.

But in order for the spirituality of work to become a reality in our lives, we have to develop a way of practicing it, a set of disciplines that we can follow right in our workplaces without people even recognizing what we are doing. These disciplines must help us discover the meaning of our work, deal with others, balance our responsibilities, decide right and wrong, and maintain and change the institutions in which we work. I call these the disciplines of the spirituality of work.

Chapter 2

How Can Work Be Spiritual?

We work because the world is unfinished
and it is ours to develop.

Joan Chittister

How much we connect to our work in a spiritual sense is determined by how we answer five major questions. These questions are the same for everyone, although the answers can be very different, based in large part on the spiritual outlook one brings to them. How we respond to these five questions is based on our spirituality, but also shapes our spirituality.

What Is the Meaning of Work?

For some, work is a way to make a living or put bread on the table. This in itself can be a spiritual reason, emphasizing responsibility, independence, stewardship, and other virtues. Just ask someone who is involuntarily unemployed or underemployed about the holiness of this aspect of work.

Other people view their work as a career or profession, one that requires special skills and training and provides a service to individuals and society. This meaning of work is not limited to white-collar jobs. Actors, artists, athletes, teachers, craftspeople, and many other workers consider their work to be something to which they have dedicated their lives. Part of the meaning they derive from their jobs includes being true to their profession or building their career.

> **We have elevated** the contemplatives' words of wisdom over those of ordinary persons, and this is the crux of the problem with the spirituality of work. Those of us engaged in the workaday world have an equal and unique contribution to make to this kind of spirituality. We have the insight from the inside out, not the outside in, and both sets of eyes are essential to see the spirit at work.
>
> **Michael Galligan-Stierle**—director of campus ministry, husband, and father Wheeling, West Virginia

Still others consider their work to be a vocation or a "call from God," a very specific type of work that they are "meant" to do. Some even claim that they would do the work whether they were paid or not. Priests and ministers are the most obvious examples of those who find this meaning in their work, but a whole variety of other people have begun to look at their work this way. As a publisher, for example, I know several people in the book and/or periodical business who believe that they are somehow called by God to do that specific work (however they understand that call to have taken place).

Besides making a living, having a career, or answering a vocation, some people find meaning in doing a good, conscientious job or providing high-quality goods or services to others. Above and beyond (and sometimes despite) their pay, these people really care about the results and effect of their work. They do good work not because someone is watching, not to keep their jobs or get a raise, not even because they feel especially

> **If, in our daily work,** we are to be cocreators of the world, we'd better be paying attention to what we are doing—questioning the value, the purpose, and the process of it, as well as the means and the ends of it.
>
> It's not easy to discern opportunities to participate in divinity with a dozen unreturned phone calls on our to-do list, a computer down, a report that's two days late, and an angry client on line three. One idea is to clarify our goals while we are away from our work. We need to think—when we are not working—about the kind of poet, printer, tradesperson, teacher, bagger, lawyer, caregiver, parking-lot attendant, president, salesperson, priest, publisher we want to be. That discipline can trigger an attitude of heightened awareness when we are back in the fray at work. How does paying attention raise our consciousness of the transcendent? They are one and the same thing.
>
> **Michael Coyne**—salesperson, husband, and father, Pittsburgh, Pennsylvania

called to the particular work they are doing. To them, it is a matter of pride—not the "I'm better than you are" kind of pride, but the pride that God must take in creation itself.

Another aspect of work is duty. People do prodigious amounts of work out of a sense of duty; there is a job to be done, so they do it. Much volunteer and family work is done for this reason. Soldiers join the army, firefighters work crazy hours, farmers work their farms long after it is financially viable, parents clean up after sick children, coaches coach other people's kids—partly, at least, out of a sense of duty.

Some love their work, others hate it, still others consider their work to be part of God's ongoing creation. All of these are examples of meaning that people find in their work, and the meaning both contributes to and is influenced by their spiritual life.

How Do We Deal with Others at Work?

Virtually no one today works alone. We all have bosses, supervisors, colleagues, employees, customers, suppliers, and competitors. How we deal with each of these groups can be an important element of our spiritual lives.

At the most basic level, we should treat others with *friendliness and common decency.* This may seem obvious, but anyone who is familiar with the modern workplace knows that these are virtues not universally practiced.

Some people consider their worklives healthy if they manage to avoid doing anything illegal, but others think that the issues of *honesty and integrity* in the workplace go much deeper.

Loyalty and encouragement are important to healthy workplace dynamics. Not only is there a perceived lack of loyalty on the part of employers, but also it is no longer safe to assume the loyalty of employees, colleagues, customers, suppliers, and others. Likewise, competition between and among people in the workplace has made the idea of encouraging or celebrating the success of others seem quaint and even somewhat soft.

Is it possible to function in the marketplace without following the survival of the fittest philosophy that is so prevalent? Or is this philosophy the only one that ensures the efficiency and health of the economy? How can *justice and generosity* become normal practice where we work? Only a spirituality of work can help us find the answers to such questions.

Several years ago, I was doing family therapy with a couple because the wife had had this great "conversion" experience and was becoming more charismatic every day. Her newfound religion was driving a wedge in their marriage. She thought that her husband, who was an outdoor electric line-man in northern Minnesota, was "nonspiritual."

At one point, I asked the man how he experienced God. In quiet, gentle tones, he told me—and his wife—about being up on an electric pole, inches away from one hundred thousand volts of electric power, looking across vast beautiful snow-covered fields. He said that in such moments he knew that God was with him and protecting him. He described how awesome God's creation is, how he gave thanks at those moments for his children, his wife, his fellow workers, his job. The wife's eyes were full of tears, as were mine. Despite her conversion experience, which was centered in a traditional religious setting, she had never really asked her husband about his spirituality, which he obviously found in his work.

We have not reflected sufficiently on both the grandeur and the degrading nature of most work in the world. We have not listened enough to the stories of holiness in ordinary life. Being immersed in daily work is a great spiritual undertaking, as profound as anything that John of the Cross or Teresa of Ávila or Ignatius Loyola ever undertook.

I worked for a CEO in a major billion-dollar state government organization several years ago who comes closer to living the spirituality of work than anyone I have known. She was direct and honest but never disparaging of others. She was strategic but not conniving. Her power came from her vision, not just from the authority she held by virtue of her position. She was gentle in her correction or direction of others—affirming but not mushy. She was passionate but not emotional, smart, tolerant of other views but always clear about her own. She always listened before deciding anything. She was able to change her mind, but she was also deeply convinced about her own values. She treated others like she wanted to be treated, and others who worked for her eventually began to behave that way too.

Timothy J. Schmaltz—social worker, teacher, writer, husband, father, and grandfather, Phoenix, Arizona

It seems to me that living in the present is the key to spirituality in all areas, but especially in the workplace. It's so easy to let the mind get distracted and to function on autopilot during work hours, particularly if our work is tedious, repetitive, or boring (as all work sometimes is). To be fully in the present moment means that we can see the value of the work we are doing at the time we are doing it. Consequently, it becomes infused with meaning.

How to do this consistently is, of course, the big question. I seem to achieve it best when I approach my work as prayer. I do not mean praying while working but considering the work itself the prayer. To think of my work—however boring, dull, or unpleasant—as prayer seems to increase my attention to detail and thus automatically increase the quality and care with which I work.

Now, if I could just do this regularly!

Woodeene Koenig-Bricker—writer, editor, and mother, Eugene, Oregon

How Do We Balance Work with the Rest of Life?

Most people have commitments to their work, to their family, to their church, to their community, and to themselves. On what basis are the decisions made about the allocation of time, energy, and resources to each of these areas?

For some people, money, power, and prestige are the primary determinants of where and how they spend their time. Others bring different values to bear on their choices—things like stability, creativity, love, and the common good.

We are all familiar with workaholics who put their job first in all circumstances. It is a disease for which there is very little negative consequence—at least in the workplace. Rather there are often real payoffs in terms of pay, promotions, and the approbation of superiors. Yet few things are less spiritual than allowing our paid employment to overwhelm our responsibilities to self and others.

But there are also people who allow their family concerns to negatively affect their work or who spend all their time on politics. Some volunteer inordinate amounts of time to church work or to work for a local charity. These last people are sometimes called "do-gooders" or "churchaholics," and rather than condemning people with such mistaken priorities, we often give them awards.

For many of us, the need to have it all is the greatest temptation. Not only do we want well-paying, interesting, responsible jobs, but we also want to be active in church and society, have a spouse and children, maintain a nice home, and so forth.

How we respond to the pressure of trying to balance all of these elements differs, but respond we all must. And our spirituality will determine how.

How Do We Determine
What Is Right and What Is Wrong?

The act of distinguishing right from wrong in the workplace is often referred to as business ethics. If something is clearly unethical at work, and especially if it is also illegal, most people simply refuse to do it. It is the gray, ambiguous questions that people have a harder time deciding. How hard should we work? How scrupulous should we be about following work and safety rules? Are customers truly always right, and if not, how are they to be treated? Most of these decisions get made on the basis of our values or priorities, which are (or should be) spiritually informed.

Then there are the sins of omission. Are there things we could be doing at work—because of our power or position, for example—that we are not doing? If so, how do we identify and act on those things? If we are successful in our work, then what do we do with success once we have it? What special responsibilities and obligations does "success" bring with it? And if we have a lower-level job, what kind of responsibilities and obligations do we have then?

Part of the problem with deciding right and wrong at work is that it depends on how much power we have. If we are lower-level workers, then there is often nothing we can do about certain situations or practices in our workplaces—unless they are so egregious that we have to blow the whistle (and take the consequences). If we are the boss or owner, our ethical responsibilities—when it comes to such issues as environmental concerns, safety, quality, compensation, and profitability—are much greater. Many people whose parents and grandparents were mostly members of the working class now hold top positions in industry, education, government, health, the military, and most other fields. Their power in the workplace now makes them much more capable of doing both good and evil than their relatives in previous generations were.

Another consideration is that people who are used to having power can sometimes take it for granted and thus ignore the ethical implications of their decisions, while people unused to having power may not have developed good skills for making decisions and setting policies. In any case, wherever we are in the hierarchy of power, we need a spirituality with which to grapple with ethical dilemmas.

How Do We Maintain—and Sometimes Change—the Workplace?

Everyone who works should be concerned about maintaining what works in the workplace and changing what doesn't. The very institutions in which we work—the banks and businesses, the government agencies, the factories and farms—must function well if we are to do our best work. Functioning well does not necessarily mean functioning in a way that is the most profitable or even the most efficient—although neither of these are bad things. Institutions that are organized

> **My experience as a** letter carrier with the U.S. Postal Service taught me that in the midst of business there can be a stillness in which God speaks and acts. So often I have had the deepest sense of God or had some revelation when I've been hard at work. My best time of prayer is when my feet are moving on my route.
>
> **Rose M. Hart**—letter carrier
> Glen Dale, West Virginia

correctly are those that enable human potential and productivity to flourish.

If the institutions in which we work function well, we must figure out how to keep them on the right path. If the institutions are dysfunctional, we must work to change them. Sometimes these transformations can be done easily and behind the scenes. Other times, they can be a controversial, messy, public process. In either case, the change must occur if we are to perform our work under the best possible conditions and in line with our deepest spiritual values.

What Spiritual Disciplines
Can Really Work in the Workplace?

Spiritual disciplines can help us address the five questions just discussed because these questions are profoundly spiritual concerns. But we need more than to merely fall back on contemplative disciplines that don't adapt easily to the workplace. (For example, learning to meditate in the midst of a busy subway, forming a Bible study group that meets over lunch, or listening to spiritual tapes in the car during your commute.) None of these contemplative practices have succeeded in attracting many people in the workplace. Certainly there are those who follow them "religiously," but they are a minority, even among practicing Christians.

> **We seldom think of** the workplace as a source of the touch of God in our lives. I have never heard a coworker say, "I just got chewed out by the boss. Boy, was that the touch of God!" However, God's presence can be experienced in the workplace. It can happen when a coworker shows appreciation for help with a project, when we are congratulated for a job well done, or when we have a sense of personal satisfaction in knowing we have done our best. It is just a matter of being aware of the source of goodness in our lives.
>
> **David Karmon**—college professor, husband, and father, Mt. Pleasant, Michigan

The fact is that disciplines of contemplative spirituality simply do not lend themselves to the contemporary workplace. The business environment values speed and efficiency; contemplation requires large blocks of time with no particular product in mind. While contemplatives ponder eternal truths, the workplace is looking for the latest innovation. Entrepreneurs are the heroes of corporate culture, while mystics are the saints of contemplative spirituality.

The disciplines of the spirituality of work, therefore, must be different from those of contemplative spirituality. What they would share, of course, is the fact that they are both sets of disciplines. That is, they are practices performed on a regular basis in order to produce expected results. Thus, with the classical spiritual disciplines someone might meditate for half an hour each morning, expecting to become calm and focused. Another might read a chapter of the Bible each day or say the same prayer morning, noon, and night to be reminded of spiritual matters.

> **I teach a humanities course** on the subject of work, and I find great resistance on the part of students to the more contemplative writers—primarily because those writers so often lack significant work experience. The students' assumption is that you can't really tell another person how to integrate work into his or her spiritual life until you have struggled with the daily grind for a significant period of time.
>
> This bias is somewhat confirmed by my experience with advice given by clergy about work. Their insights were long on generalities and short on specifics, in large part because all they had ever known was work within the church. Most of them had never tried to implement their faith in a hostile work setting.
>
> **David B. Raymond**—college instructor
> Mapleton, Maine

The disciplines of a spirituality of work would have to be like these traditional disciplines, yet be designed for today's busy workplace. They would have to be new disciplines, not mere adaptations of contemplative disciplines. They would have to be practices that could be done in the workplace without disrupting the flow of the work.

They would have to be things that people who are not particularly pious, or even religious, would feel comfortable doing.

What are these disciplines? I don't have a definite answer, but I have started practicing a few in recent years, and I have been talking with others who have developed disciplines of their own, many of which are included on these pages. I offer the disciplines described here only as a starting point for discussion. They would have to be judged not only on how they make the practitioners feel but also on how well those who practice the disciplines affect and transform the workplace itself. For the litmus test for all spirituality is twofold: it must both raise practitioners' consciousness of the divine presence yet also increase their commitment to making the world a better place. (Think of the Our Father: "Thy kingdom come, thy will be done, on earth as it is in heaven.")

How do we allow the transcendent, the holy, the divine, the eternal that is already present everywhere and in everything to break through to our consciousness on a regular basis? What's more, how do we accomplish this task not away from the hustle and bustle of life but rather in the midst of our daily work, with all of its accompanying stresses, deadlines, competition, injustice, and so forth? And, finally, how do we use disciplines that flow from our work and workplaces themselves, rather than trying to adapt traditional contemplative practices?

Our criteria in developing these "disciplines of the spirituality of work" will be as follows:

1. **We must be able to practice the discipline in the workplace.** Whether we work in an office, a factory, a field, a home, a church, a hotel, a vehicle, or a tollbooth, the discipline must be available to us at work. We should not have to leave our workplace to find God.

2. **We must be able to practice the discipline without disrupting our work.** If the spirituality of work becomes a distraction or a

detriment to our performance, it will be counterproductive and soon abandoned.

3. **We must be able to practice the discipline regularly and consistently.** This may mean hourly, daily, weekly, monthly, quarterly, yearly, or on some other schedule.

4. **The discipline must be triggered by some event, task, or situation that occurs in the workplace.** In other words, we must rely on something to remind us to practice the discipline rather than rely on ourselves to remember to "be spiritual."

5. **We must be able to practice the discipline without anyone in the workplace knowing that we are doing so.** It is not that what we are doing won't be noticed or that if asked we would deny our spiritual motivation, but rather it must be that we give not the slightest hint of being self-righteous or holier than thou. We should follow Jesus' advice, "When you pray, do so behind closed doors."

So, join me on a journey of discovery. If there is a spirituality of work, it must be disciplined, and if we can discover and practice the disciplines, then our work will indeed be spiritual.

Chapter 3

Surrounding Yourself with Sacred Objects

They maintain the fabric of this world,
and the practice of their craft is their prayer.

Sirach 38:34

The first discipline of the spirituality of work may seem a little pious. It may even remind us of more traditional spirituality. But it can meet the five criteria outlined at the end of chapter two, and it can be practiced inside the most secular of workplaces.

This discipline is to surround ourselves with "sacred objects." A sacred object can be anything from a piece of traditional religious art to a photo of family and friends, or it can be some completely secular item that carries for us a very deep and spiritual meaning. Some people even refer to their collection of objects as an altar, but most are content to merely have them around, without necessarily assigning religious words or titles to them.

Journalist Mary Beth Sammons offers an example of people who surround themselves with sacred objects in their workplaces. "If God speaks to us in the details of our everyday lives, then Chicago trial lawyer Michael Coffield is hearing the message," she says. She describes the walls of Coffield's office: "Brimming from glass shelves lining the wall are the holy relics—mementos—of his family and faith life." Among the mementos are many giraffes. "I'm fascinated

On a bulletin board over my desk I have a tiny note with two simple images drawn on it—a cross and a fish. That evokes for me the simplicity of the early Christians. Remember those childhood stories of our forebears drawing a fish in the dirt to identify themselves to other believers?

I have been a nurse for almost twenty-five years. I've been privileged to be with people during intimate times in their lives (birth, death, and in between). For me, spirituality is making an effort to see the individuality of people, listening to them, putting them at ease, and treating them with respect. This can mean looking beyond an unpleasant appearance or smell or a whining, grating voice.

I have worked in both hospitals and offices, and I have found that the more I have practiced the Golden Rule the greater the benefits I have received in turn. Health care may be the ideal environment in which to practice this discipline.

Cathlin Buckingham Poronsky—family nurse practitioner, wife, and mother
Western Springs, Illinois

by giraffes because they teach me many spiritual lessons," says Coffield. "They're tall enough to see over the crowds and they're wise enough to look through the jungle and trees and see what really is going on before they make any moves, and only then do they take gentle action. . . . When I lose focus in all the busyness, these things reconnect me to my inner beliefs and my faith. They help me center."

In her book *Altars Made Easy: A Complete Guide to Creating Your Own Sacred Space,* author Peg Streep notes: "Carving out a bit of sacred space in the [workplace]—no matter how small or unobtrusive—is an important reminder that the various dualisms or bifurcations our society encourages us to believe in—the separation of the sacred and the profane, the intellect and the spirit, the mind and the body, the professional and the personal—are really not helpful if we intend to live productive, fulfilled, and spiritually rewarding lives. By creating sacred space where we work, we signify our presence there and our intention to use the time we spend at work as fruitfully as possible."

My own office is full of sacred objects. First and foremost are the pictures of my family—both nuclear and extended. They are the most important people in my life, and they provide my work with both purpose and meaning. By that I mean that the pictures remind me that one of the many reasons I am working is to make a living, so that I can help provide my family with the material things we need (and many that we merely desire). The photos of my friends and family are also my first ring of contact with all the people—employees, colleagues, customers, competitors—that my work touches. They make me realize that my work—and how I do it—is important to other people.

Other sacred objects in my office include the plaques of the dozen or more children's baseball teams I have coached in the last few years. They are an immediate source of joy and pride, but they also serve to keep my work in perspective. Yes, my job is important, but it is ultimately not any more important than some of the other work I do away from the workplace—most often for no pay.

As a special-education teacher, I deal with behaviorally and emotionally disturbed children, mildly mentally retarded children, children who have severe hyperactive and attention deficits, children who have horrid family lives and sometimes horrid school experiences, and children who are behind in their work for some unknown reason.

In the beginning of my career about eight years ago, I would go home and weep for these kids, but then as I began to pray about the challenge of how to deal with them and not lose hope for them myself, I began to rethink my whole approach. I now have found the great difference between pity and compassion.

So instead of worrying about what each day will bring, I bought a simple prayer card and placed it on my desk. It is called "St. Patrick's Breast-Plate," and on it are the words "Christ before me . . . Christ behind me . . . Christ in every person who thinks of me . . . Christ in every person who hears me . . . " Every morning as the kids come in and begin to get ready for the day, I sit quietly and look to see who is in front of me, behind me, listening to me, speaking to me, etc. It gives me a whole new perspective every day. I regret the days when I forget to look at my prayer card or don't make time for it. I may not know why I was not pleased with my performance for the day, but the next day when I'm going through the prayer I suddenly am reminded that I did not focus on what my real mission was the day before.

My best friend gave me a beautiful icon of Michael the Archangel as a Native American. It is so beautiful, yet it is hard to imagine without seeing it. He gave me a large one for my home but also a small one for my desk at the school. (Since I'm a public school teacher he didn't think I could put religious icons and such on my desk. However, the school athletic mascot is an Indian, so no one noticed!) What is interesting is how the kids are always drawn to the plaque. There is nothing about it that makes it look like anything other than an ordinary picture, but maybe the children see what adults are blind to.

These two items—a prayer card and a plaque—are the only items on my desk of any religious nature. Around them I place the kids' pictures, the little things they give me, and so forth. They make a special place that I created somewhat intentionally as a way of reminding myself of the deeper meaning of my work.

Doreen M. Badeaux—special-education teacher, Port Arthur, Texas

I have a small collection of old metal printer's blocks in my office. These are beautiful objects in themselves, and they keep me aware that my work is but a small chapter in a long story of the publishing profession. In addition, they comfort me as I try to keep up with all the changes in technology in my business, because they are concrete reminders that technological innovation is both a normal part of work and a part of God's ongoing plan of creation.

I have artwork in my office—most of it by artists I have met, and all of it evocative of issues that I do not want to forget as I go about my daily work. I do have two pieces of religious art. One is a crucifix made out of scrap metal by a Haitian artist, and the other is a bronze Celtic cross made in Ireland. I also have a printout over my computer that plays off the famous slogan "It's the economy, stupid" that hung in the Bill Clinton campaign headquarters years ago. Mine says simply, "It's the Incarnation, stupid."

> **I try to make the desk** in my office an altar on which I celebrate the liturgy of my work. If you extend the metaphor, the office becomes a sanctuary and my fellow workers then concelebrate the liturgy with me. This practice doesn't succeed as often as I'd like, but when it does, it is really wonderful.
>
> **William H. Farley**—commercial real estate developer, husband, father, and grandfather Hartford, Connecticut

The Purpose of Keeping Sacred Objects

The purpose of keeping these sacred objects in my workplace is simply to catch myself up short, to distract myself for a moment, to keep me in touch, if you will, with transcendental reality. Except for the crucifixes and the printout, my sacred objects are not pious or religious in the traditional sense of those words. Most people would not even categorize them as spiritual. Yet they are to me.

The discipline is for me to be open to these sacred objects and willing to let them break into my life at any time. It's not that I have to spend much time with them. Sometimes I only give them a fleeting thought; sometimes they might lead to a short meditation or prayer. Most of the time they are merely part of the background of my workplace.

One special object that has recently joined my workplace collection is a small tin box that says "Old-Time Baseball" and has on its lid a painting of a couple of players from a previous era. This tin was given to me by one of my authors. It had belonged to her seventeen-year-old son, who committed suicide just days before her first book was scheduled to go to the printer. At the author's request, I was able to change the dedication of the book to her son, and it meant a lot to her. Knowing my love for baseball and children, she wanted me to have the tin in which her son kept his favorite baseball cards.

Every time I look at this object it causes me to think about the ultimate meaning of life, this family's sorrow, and the despair that the boy must have felt. I say a quick prayer for my own children and go on with my work, always just a little more aware of its importance and of God's presence in the work I do.

Sacred Objects in Secular Settings

You might argue that this discipline is easy for some people to practice but impossible for others. It might be possible for school teachers or office managers or homemakers to surround themselves with sacred objects, but what about police officers or waitresses or construction workers? Some people work in environments that are hostile to any display of spirituality or even of personal preference or identity.

The answers to these situations may lie in creativity and miniaturization. A lawyer's briefcase may have to be plain on the outside, but no court in the country would object if a personal picture or item were inside. Some people may have to display their sacred objects in the car in which they commute rather than in the place in which they work. Almost every parent carries pictures in a purse or wallet with no objection from his or her employer. The tollbooth operator or fast-food worker may be able to have only one small object that can be placed unobtrusively by a cash register during their shift. Perhaps this object needs to be changed daily, or maybe that one object has to carry the entire spiritual load every day.

Traditional religious practices might offer some ideas here. Some people still bow their heads or make the sign of the cross as they pass a church. Perhaps people who spend most of their work time in vehicles could develop similar habits. (It might not be churches that inspire the thought of the presence of God, however. It could just as well be the sirens of emergency vehicles, four-way stop signs, or other everyday objects to which special meaning is assigned.) The practice of wearing a medal or lapel pin might also be adapted to the spirituality of work. A chain with or without an object attached, a pin or earring, a special belt buckle, even a watch could become a sacred object for anyone who chooses to make it so.

Another option might be to turn secular objects into sacred objects. No workplace can object to a magazine or a daily newspaper. Perhaps a page of the periodical—a particular column, section, or topic—can serve as the trigger to our becoming conscious of the presence of God that day. We could be riding the bus or subway with a sacred object in full view in our hands, and no one would even suspect!

Even books can become sacred objects. Show me an employer who bans employees from bringing books to work, and I'll call the ACLU for you. We don't have to read the book at work, just carry it there and be aware of its presence. It doesn't even have to be a book on spiritual matters to remind us that—bidden or not—God is present in our workplace.

> **Having sacred objects** surrounding us in the workplace is an important reminder that the various dualisms in our lives are really not helpful if we want to lead full spiritual lives. The shopping mall, the school, the kitchen table, the courtroom, the factory, and the office can be altars of sorts—places where the mundane labors of life may be offered up, blessed, and transformed into things of beauty and holiness.
>
> **William Droel**—college instructor, campus minister, husband, and father
> Chicago, Illinois

If we practice this discipline regularly over a long period of time (which is part of the definition of a discipline), then we might find that our sacred objects have become so familiar that we stop noticing them. Then it's time to refresh them. This could mean getting some new objects. Introducing a new sacred object into the workplace can revitalize this entire practice. Not only does the new object remind us to be more aware of the spirituality of our work, it often serves to renew the power of our other sacred objects.

A variation on this is a new discipline I began a couple of years ago. At the end of the year—after Christmas and before New Year's Day—I clean my office. This might not sound like such a big deal, but my desk is almost always a disaster area, as any of my coworkers will confirm. Not only does this annual cleaning make my office much nicer (more like the way God would have things?) for myself and others, it also has had an unintended result. As I clean and move all my sacred objects around once a year, I find that I notice them anew and that this noticing lasts for many months.

Inside my coat closet—a personal space in the classroom of the public school where I teach—I pasted on the door that bracing verse from John 11, the words Martha uses to call Mary to Jesus' side: "The teacher is here and is calling for you." Since my work is often discouraging and exhausting, I find that I sometimes need to be reminded that my work is a calling, even a privilege.

Julie Drew—elementary school teacher and mother, Evanston, Illinois

---

My office is filled with photos of gardens, flowers, mountains, impressionist prints and family pictures. They surround me as reminders of the beauty of creation and help me see the beauty in all that I do. If someone wants to call them altars, it's OK by me. Maybe the image of altar is the interactions between each other and between us and God. I don't use such religious terminology. I prefer just to call my pictures the "stuff" of each day.

Michael Nachman—educator and diocesan administrator, husband, father, and grandfather, Madison, Wisconsin

A final idea for refreshing our sacred objects is to transform an annoying object into a sacred one. This is actually quite simple. One woman I know was constantly irritated at work by the ringing of her phone. After thinking about it for a while, she decided to make her telephone a sacred object. Every time it rings, she tries to remember to think that it is God calling. When this practice becomes too familiar, she changes the volume or type of ring and finds that this renews the effect for many days.

Practicing the Discipline

- Start with one sacred object. Take it to your workplace, and each time you notice it, become aware of the deeper spiritual meaning of your work.

- Add other sacred objects to your workplace one at a time as appropriate. Do not add another until the originals have begun to lose their effectiveness. If it is difficult to have many objects in your workplace at one time, replace or alternate your sacred object(s) as needed.

- Try to wear a sacred object unobtrusively.

- Turn a secular object in your workplace into a sacred object.

- Find or designate one sacred object that you pass or encounter each day in your work or on your commute to work.

- Move your sacred objects at work around daily, weekly, monthly, or yearly as needed.

Chapter 4

Living with Imperfection

Authentic work connects us to the creative habits
of the universe.

Thomas Aquinas

Cardinal John Henry Newman once said that nothing would ever be done if we waited until we could do it so perfectly that no one could find fault with it. The second spiritual discipline of work is based on making a positive out of a negative. The negative is that we all make mistakes in our work. The positive is that we can find God in the midst of them.

There is a Sufi story of a woman who went into a marketplace, looked around, and saw a sign that read *God's Fruit Stand*. "Thank goodness," the woman said to herself. "It's about time!"

She went inside and said to God, "I would like a perfect banana, a perfect cantaloupe, a perfect strawberry, and a perfect peach."

Standing behind the counter, God merely shrugged and said, "I'm sorry, I sell only seeds."

Even God leaves it to us to develop, however imperfectly, the potential in our work and in ourselves.

> Part of the process of rejecting perfectionism involves accepting that things don't always happen as we plan or as we would like. We might wish to be in control—imposing our own notions of order on the universe—but we're not. Change happens, and flexibility is a key to dealing with it spiritually.
>
> **Sheila Denion**—businessperson, educator, and wife, West Hartford, Connecticut

> Have you heard about Navajo weavers who weave an imperfection into every rug to let the spirit breathe? In any work of art it is the "mistakes" that open the way to directions that would never have been discovered. Being comfortable with the expectation of imperfections and being open to the spirit in them is the only climate for creativity. These are the locked doors of the soul: fear of trying, needing a "right" answer, fear of the new, seeing failure as an end rather than a beginning.
>
> **Jean Morman Unsworth**—artist, art educator, author, and wife Chicago, Illinois

Getting Out the Last Typos

When I first became an editor, I went to a seminar where the instructor said that every book published should have two typographical errors. The idea was that the amount of work it would take to get those last two typos out of a manuscript was not worth it. Editors just had to live with imperfection if they were going to accomplish anything.

That was a very liberating lesson for me—and not just in my editing work. I am very much an imperfect editor, parent, spouse, coach, community organizer, and church volunteer. I have to learn to live with it, and living with imperfection is one of the disciplines within the spirituality of work that I now practice.

The beauty of this particular discipline is that we don't have to do much to remember to practice it. Most of the time, our imperfection rises up and confronts us, and if it doesn't, our bosses (or colleagues or spouses or children or friends or neighbors) are quick to point it out to us. All we need do to practice this discipline is build into the workday concrete ways of accepting that we are not perfect. (For example, every time I find a typo in one of the books I publish, I give glory to God.)

> **If I cannot be tolerant** of my own faults, how can I tolerate those of others? On the other hand, I cannot tolerate those faults of mine that get in the way of my doing my job. A surgeon friend of mine, despite still being very good at his work, is planning to phase into another career prior to having to be concerned with the "ravages of aging" on his skills. This is both professional and humble.
>
> **Thomas A. Bausch**—professor of management, husband, father, and grandfather
> Milwaukee, Wisconsin

Overrating Perfection

The idea that our work can be perfect is, on the face of it, absurd. Part of the very nature of humanity is our imperfection. On the few occasions that a man or woman achieves perfection, we call it genius and the accomplishment a masterpiece. But for most people most of the time, our work will be less than perfect—less, even, than what we are capable of in our best moments.

Does its inherent imperfection make our work less spiritual? Not necessarily. If we accept imperfection as part of the human condition, then we should be able to celebrate our failures as well as our successes. In fact, the opposite of this discipline is a sin called *perfectionism.* Out of our egotism and insecurity, we try to do the impossible—that is, be perfect—with the predictable result that we make a mess of the very work we are trying to accomplish, we drive our colleagues crazy, and we harm our spiritual life in the process.

In his book *Protect Us from All Anxiety: Meditations for the Depressed,* Fr. William Burke describes the problem with trying to be a perfectionist: "A perfectionist is ill, trying desperately to live an impossible life." Burke then goes on to make this prayer: "Lord, I hate the imperfect in me. I despise it. I want to hide it. Which means I hate, despise, and want to hide me. Yet you love me. Something's got to give."

People in the arts and in sports learn quickly how to live with imperfection. What concert does not contain a wrong note, and what painting could not be improved with more work? Yet the artist must at some point let go, or no communication would take place, no beauty would be observed. The best hitters in all of baseball fail six out of ten times, and even ESPN's Athlete of the Century, Michael Jordan, missed shots and made mental errors. Athletes and artists are great precisely because they are imperfect, not despite it. People in fact reach greater heights of performance because they push the envelope and risk greater failure and imperfection. Imperfection is a condition of growth, and athletes and artists know that if they don't push beyond what they have already achieved they cannot do their best work. The same is true for each of us.

> **Excellence makes** no pretense of striving for perfection, which can never occur. We have no notion of what perfection is, and therefore we are incapable of achieving it. Excellence, on the other hand, is achievable and measurable. As new levels of excellence become possible, new standards can be adopted according to our abilities and personal standards.
>
> **Leo T. Bistak**—diocesan director of evangelization and deacon formation, husband, and father, Toledo, Ohio

Living with the Imperfection of Others

While we may be able to train ourselves to accept our own imperfection, learning to live with the imperfection of others in the workplace can be even more daunting. We count on others to do their work correctly, and we are justifiably irritated when they do not. The discipline of living with imperfection, however, forces us to take a step back and reconsider before we issue a complaint or a reprimand.

The first consideration is the importance of the mistake. If it is a matter of safety—the proper functioning or operation of an automobile or a nuclear generator, for example—then certainly there can't be much tolerance for error. We can be more accepting of error when someone gets our lunch order wrong or when the bus is late. Mathematics and astronomy require much more precision than most of our occupations. We all know people who overreact to the mistakes and failures of others. They seem to almost enjoy finding fault in the work of others and are quick to point it out. I have not, however, found these people to be noticeably more in tune with the Creator than the rest of us.

A second question we have to ask ourselves when we encounter the imperfection of others is why these lapses are occurring. If it is a matter of sloth or inattention or lack of caring, then it is difficult to see anything spiritual about that imperfection. But if someone is doing less than perfect work because he or she is exhausted from caring for a sick friend or relative, then that fact might shed an entirely different light on the person's minor failures. Similarly, can we really expect perfect work from someone who is being unjustly exploited in terms of pay or working conditions? Or perhaps a worker was momentarily distracted by the real needs of another colleague or a customer. Aren't those good enough reasons to make a mistake?

There are hundreds of legitimate reasons someone might make an error. A new employee might be learning the job. An older employee might be losing a step to age. An engaged or newly married person might be daydreaming momentarily about his or her beloved. Think of all the reasons we have been less than perfect in our work; we can compile our own list of explanations. Did these occasions mean that we were bad workers or out of touch with God's creative energy? In some cases, the very acts of imperfection proved how wonderfully human we were.

The discipline of living with imperfection is merely a daily carrying out of the words of the Our Father, which—loosely translated—might be "forgive us our imperfections, as we forgive the imperfections of others."

Discovering the Spirituality of Imperfection

There are several ways that the discipline of living with our imperfection gets us in touch with God in our lives. First, it reminds us of our human frailty and it relieves us of any idea that we can bring about God's work on our own, without divine help. This seems to me to be partly what angered Jesus so much about the religious leaders he encountered. They somehow thought that they could be perfect in their observance of the Law, rather than recognize and accept that they too were imperfect.

Living with our imperfection also gives us perspective

Can I be less than perfect and still count myself as a good person? Can I feel good about my efforts (work, family, and community) if they fall short? The struggle with accepting imperfection in our lives might be related to the messages we hear starting with the word *should*. And possibly the worst "should" is that we need to be perfect like God is perfect. What a load to carry! Maybe we need to learn that we are not God and that not being God is OK. In fact, it is great!

I suggest two approaches to imperfection: 1) Living in the present and doing the best we can with the task at hand, then moving on to the next effort. To do this, we have to give up some of our control and believe that others have something to contribute. 2) Being humble enough to allow someone else to apply their imperfection to a task, hopefully resulting in something a little less imperfect than if we had done it entirely by ourselves.

Michael Nachman—educator and diocesan administrator, husband, father, and grandfather, Madison, Wisconsin in our work. It helps us realize that work is not the only important thing in life, that we have other responsibilities to balance with our work. (If it would take me fifteen hours to get those last few typos out of a book, that is fifteen hours I must take away from something or someone else in my busy life. See the chapter on balancing work, personal, family, church, and community responsibilities.)

Finally—and this is its most radical aspect—living with our imperfection may help us understand and accept God's "imperfection." One of the favorite Scripture passages of perfectionists is "You must be perfect, even as your heavenly Father is perfect." This is usually taken as an injunction to do better and better, but if you think about it, creation itself has a lot of "typos" in it. (Woody Allen once commented that if God is all powerful, he certainly is an underachiever.)

The obvious fact is, of course, that creation is an ongoing process and that for whatever reason—and who can know the mind of God?—creation keeps happening, at least partly, through the imperfect work of human hands and minds. So by living with our own imperfection, we are being "perfect" in the way that our heavenly Father is perfect—not in the sense of making no mistakes or leaving nothing undone but rather in the sense of being perfect in purity of intention and honesty of effort. The discipline of living with our own imperfection reminds us daily that we are an integral part of God's ongoing creation, that we are charged with helping the "reign of God come, on earth as it is in heaven."

> **Imperfection is hard** to address, since I wallow in it. Thérèse of Lisieux, our most recent Doctor of the Church, was the expert on weaving a spirituality of imperfection. If ever there was a ragged soul of pettiness and selfishness, it was hers. Yet she didn't let her admittedly spoiled personality interfere with her progress in the Spirit. For sheer persistence against the odds, we canonized her.
>
> **Alice L. Camille**—writer and lay minister
> Berkeley, California

Practicing the Discipline

- Pick one thing in your work that is equivalent to leaving a couple of typos in a book. Adopt this imperfection as a goal, share it publicly with others, and celebrate it when it occurs.

- Make a list of all the good reasons you do imperfect work. Put the list where you will see it regularly—on your mirror at home or on your computer at work. Add to the list whenever you come up with a new valid reason for imperfection.

- Each time you encounter imperfection in the work of another, stop for a moment and reflect on the humanness you share with that person and the various valid choices he or she may have made to allow the imperfection to occur.

> **What does it mean to be perfect?**
>
> Only God is perfect. God is God—and I am not. I am human—created, dependent, imperfect, and all the rest. All I can do is the best that I can with what God has given me to do it with. I cannot (and certainly, God cannot) expect any more than that. To do so would drive me (and everyone around me) crazy and threaten any potential I might have to understand how much God loves me.
>
> **John Ulrich, OFM**—Catholic priest and pastor, member of religious community Boston, Massachusetts

- Before you criticize the imperfections of others in your workplace, say a quick Our Father, substituting the words "forgive us our imperfections, as we forgive the imperfections of others."

- Each time you go to an art or sporting event, look for one imperfection and give thanks for it.

- Say Fr. Burke's prayer of imperfection each day: "Lord, I hate the imperfect in me. I despise it. I want to hide it. Which means I hate, despise, and want to hide me. Yet you love me. Something's got to give."

Chapter 5

Assuring Quality

If a man is called to be a street sweeper, he should sweep
streets even as Michelangelo painted, or Beethoven com-
posed music, or Shakespeare wrote poetry. He should
sweep streets so well that all the host of heaven and earth
will pause to say, "There lived a great street sweeper who
did his job well."

Martin Luther King Jr.

While it is well and good—spiritual even—to live with our imperfection, we can never use that as an excuse for doing less than our best work. Is this a contradiction? Not entirely. Our best work, for the most part, will be imperfect. Yet, if our work is to be worthy of feeding our spiritual lives and incarnating God in the world, it must be of the best quality of which we are capable.

The success of the comic strip *Dilbert* is one cultural indicator that quality in the workplace is not to be taken for granted. "To assure quality in my work," says campus minister Tom Holahan, "I attempt each day to cry out (to myself) 'eradicate cynicism!' It is only in an atmosphere of trust and hope that I can begin the quality-assuring process."

Writer Paul Wilkes tells a story of working with his carpenter father. The two of them were laying a wood floor. It had been a long day, and the younger Wilkes was eager to quit. There was a last piece of molding to install under a radiator. It wouldn't go in right, but the young man started pounding in the finishing nails anyhow. His father stopped him. The boy pointed out that the radiator would cover the piece and that no one would ever see whether it was well fashioned or not. "They might not know, Butch," the older man said, "but you always will."

It is this idea of quality as a value in itself that forms the basis for this discipline of the spirituality of work. If we are to be truly "cocreators" with God, then our work matters, and the term we use for this is *quality*. What is difficult, however, is not the ideal, or goal, of quality but the practices we develop in order to do a good job.

Doing a Good Job

Many people experience "job satisfaction." We know when we have done good work, and we feel good about it. There is a very real spiritual sense that we are somehow attuned to a greater good, a transcendent reality. Parents, for example, get this feeling when their child graduates or gets married or does something fine. My wife loves to garden, and nothing gives her greater joy than getting her fingernails dirty and working up a good sweat planting a vegetable or flower garden.

In the marketplace, this same kind of satisfaction can occur despite—and even partially because of—low pay, difficult working conditions, or danger. Teachers and tailors, bellhops and barbers, firefighters and flight attendants—people in almost all kinds of jobs—know that when they do their work with care and skill they gain at least a glimpse of how their work serves others or the greater good.

To practice the spirituality of work in these situations, we can notice our satisfaction in a job well done, be thankful for the opportunity to do the work, and enjoy the moment, while recognizing that not all of our daily work is immediately rewarding. There are many disciplines we could adopt to accomplish this task. We might have a definite time of day when we reflect on the goodness of our work. It may be in the morning, when we make a "morning offering" of our day's work to God. It may

Because I am a human-services provider (speech therapist) and an employee, there is much in the nature of my work that I have no control over (working conditions, for example) or that is beyond my current understanding (the nature and extent of brain damage, for instance). Nevertheless, I do take my responsibilities and the quality of my work very seriously—even spiritually.

For many years, I worked with adults with mental retardation. Quality assurance was a big deal in those agencies, largely because of the abuse people with mental retardation suffered at the hands of people in power. But lack of quality assurance was not the historical problem; evil was. As a provider, I have come to the conclusion that to not do my best, to not report the reportable, to not be thorough and careful and kind or to be sloppy, careless, perfunctory, or rude to the people and their families that I serve is not just a lack of quality. It is just wrong.

I acknowledge that I will have bad days. I will get tired and discouraged. But my Christian faith has been the major support for my professional practice of assuring the quality of my work. There has been little else in my various workplaces that has given me the same motivation. (God knows that much time devoted to "quality assurance" in most work environments is spent calculating how little we can get away with doing, spending, writing, providing, and so on.)

Maureen McCarron—speech therapist, wife, and mother, Conesus, New York

I feel that "enough is enough" works when looking at basic career or lifestyle choices. I do not think it fits when it comes to the work one is doing. I have found that enough is never enough when it comes to doing a job better, more effectively, more efficiently, or with greater passion and commitment. I practice the action/reflection model of quality assurance. I find that daily reflection combined with curiosity and the desire to make a difference results in continually changing and improving the work I do. I take great satisfaction in how I do my job overall, but this discipline continually helps me find room to do it better.

At my workplace, our department is trying to shift how we do things. We are trying to move away from disconnected activities to work that connects to our larger strategy and goals. In essence, we ask ourselves whether our work is producing the results we intend. If we value our time, skills, and energy, then we want to make sure that what we do in our daily work makes a difference to the people we serve.

Assuring the quality of our work is always an interesting challenge. I find the word used so much that it has almost lost meaning. However, providing a quality product or service is important since it is a clear expression of how we value our clients, customers, or constituents. In that sense, quality is spiritual. It requires discipline, continuous review, and reflection. I think it is critical that quality assurance becomes part of how we do business and is not relegated to a special department or program. When we have to spend money to hire a quality-assurance person or team to check our products or audit our services, then we are already in trouble. Everyone within an organization must be responsible for the quality of his or her work, and we all have to check on each other.

Mark Linder—municipal department director and husband
Santa Cruz, California

be at noon, when church bells or lunch sirens ring out. Or it may be on the commute home. Some people I know keep a "work journal" in which they record the good (as well as the bad) things that happen on their jobs. Or we might just maintain a list of "blessings" our job brings us. These kinds of practices can lead to another discipline, that of giving thanks and congratulations to others and to ourselves, which is the topic of the next chapter.

Getting "Goofy" about Quality

Let's go back to the typographical errors I mentioned in the previous chapter. While it is true that I should not be "goofy" about proofreading and that I should live with my imperfection, it is not true that I should be publishing books with lots of typos. This isn't fair to my customers, my colleagues, or myself. If my company's spirituality (can a company have a spirituality?) is based in part on the work that we do, then the quality of the products and services we provide is an integral part of that spirituality. How can we maintain that our work has transcendent importance and then not try to make it the best work of which we are capable?

Business executive and author Bill Diehl, who has been instrumental in promoting the "ministry of daily life" in the Lutheran church, gives this example. "There are two ways I can assure greater quality in

> **Sometimes I go on** "personal perfection campaigns"—nothing less than 100 percent is good enough. I generally don't impose such a standard on others, only on myself. It is a sure path to burnout.
>
> Other times I merely try to "do better than anyone else" (at least better than anyone in my immediate vicinity). I find this is often another name for accepting mediocrity in my work.
>
> Occasionally, I strike a balance between cost effectiveness and personal excellence and professionalism (whatever that is). In these cases, 80 percent may be good enough for the purposes of the task, while the last 20 percent would cost far too much in terms of time, money, and sanity.
>
> **Celeste Francis**—management information systems consultant, Los Angeles, California

my secretary's typing. First, I can ask that she proofread each letter twice. The trade-off is that she would be less productive, but she could reduce her typing error rate from one in every eighty pages to perhaps one in every hundred. Second, I could proofread every memo or letter she types. Here there is a *big* trade-off. I am not using my time on work for which I have been hired, and my secretary becomes paranoid knowing I am checking all her work. Perhaps we could reduce the error rate to one in a hundred and ten pages, not so much due to my proofreading skills as to her being more careful herself before showing her work to me. So the question is, how much quality assurance can we strive for without getting 'goofy' about it?"

This is the practice that Diehl has decided upon: "One typo in every eighty pieces of correspondence is 'good enough' for my outgoing mail, but one in eighty pages of book manuscript is not. Here I will pay for two proofreaders.

> **I like the simple practice** of making sure we come to work rested and prepared. I don't think this can be assumed anymore in today's work environment, yet how important it is. I wonder how often this simple idea is stated in company employment policies. How would we feel about a heart surgeon or pilot who has had only four hours of sleep the night before or has not received any continuing education recently?
>
> **Richard M. Stojak**—diocesan family-life director, husband, father, and grandfather Keller, Texas

This is not efficient use of resources perhaps, but shouldn't we be more 'goofy' about books than about letters?"

What Is "Assuring Quality"?

Music teacher Mary Bickel points out that "the word *quality* in many contexts needs a qualifier, such as 'good' or 'high.'" She offers some practices that can lead to high-quality work: "Put in the necessary time to make our work excellent. Don't worry that some colleagues seem not to care or act as if quality doesn't matter. Think of our work as a gift to others."

However, businesswoman Sheila Denion warns, "We need to establish realistic time frames for our work, and quality standards must be realistic. Although shoddy work is unacceptable, perfectionism is a real trap. There is no 'enough' for a perfectionist. We need to accept our limitations and imperfections, even while trying conscientiously and consistently to do the best we can under the circumstances. The basic trade-offs are time and money versus quality. Where the stakes are high (for example, where life or health or safety is involved), quality cannot be sacrificed to gain time or money. Where the stakes are low (for example, typos in a daily newspaper), quality may be sacrificed for cost or timeliness considerations."

There have been many attempts to institute "quality assurance" in the workplace, and these attempts themselves can be disciplines of the spirituality of work. But whether a formal program exists or not, it is up to each of us to find a way to remind ourselves that the quality of our work—and that of others—matters, both in the simple day-to-day satisfaction of customers and in the cosmic effort to make creation an ever-better endeavor.

Perhaps assuring quality means reviewing our work one more time. How many of our mistakes and errors could be eliminated by a simple second check? This doesn't necessarily mean spending a lot more time on a project, but it might mean being more aware or careful of what we have done. If the employees at fast-food restaurants would just look in a bag one more time before handing it to a customer, how many more orders would be correct and customers happy?

In order to be more careful at work, we might have to make sure that we come to work rested and prepared. This is not as easy as it may seem. Most of us are trying to balance multiple responsibilities; of course we get tired and stressed out. If we carry this into our workplaces, however, we can end up doing slipshod work or at least work that is of a lower quality than we are capable. So perhaps getting a good night's rest or saying "no" to a social engagement or volunteer work can be holy in itself.

Assuring the quality of our work may also involve submitting to peer group review or listening more attentively to superiors. At times this can be difficult, frustrating, embarrassing, and even counterproductive, but if it is seen in the light of the spirituality of work, then we can approach it with a different attitude. The same can be said of various formal and informal training programs in the workplace.

The key to developing quality spirituality is to bring quality to the forefront of our daily work.

Practicing the Discipline

• Make a list of the various "blessings" that your work brings you. Spend a few minutes each month updating that list. As you do so, reflect on the quality you are putting into your work.

• Find one time every day—preferably a time that is noted by a sound or daily occurrence of some kind—to say a short prayer of thanksgiving for the good work you have done or will do that day.

• Figure out a practice that you can do by yourself to decrease the number of "typos" in your work. Try it for a month, then analyze the results, make adjustments, and try again for another month.

One discipline I think is essential in maintaining "quality-with-imperfection" is caring—caring for ourselves, for the earth, for the people we serve. We are more likely to work "carefully" and therefore maintain high quality in our work when we practice this discipline. When I train colleagues, such as secretaries and student assistants, I try to instill the understanding that we should all care for our constituents—administrators, faculty, students, support staff. Therefore, we need to do our jobs well and to the best of our abilities as much as possible without error.

I am not obsessed with perfection, but it is important to me that a letter does not have any typos, a label is straight on an envelope, stuff is filed where it is supposed to be. I've been indoctrinated with "If it's worth doing, it's worth doing well" since birth. It is a tape that continues to play in my head.

Doris J. Rudy—realtor, widow, and mother
Evanston, Illinois

- Work with a colleague to develop a new, informal, quality-assurance technique between the two of you. Try it for a month. Then analyze the results together, make adjustments, and try again for another month.

- After you have developed and tested a quality-assurance practice, try to get it adopted as a policy or procedure in your workplace. (See the chapter on working to make the system work.)

Chapter 6

Giving Thanks and Congratulations

In my kitchen's noise and clatter, while several people are all calling for different things, I possess God just as peacefully as if I were on my knees at the altar, ready to take communion.

Brother Lawrence

"Your thanks are in the paycheck" seems to be the attitude in many workplaces, where people are expected to perform day in and day out at very high levels of speed and competency without being thanked or congratulated for their effort. Offering thanks or congratulations, however, is a specific discipline within the spirituality of work. If it is done on a regular basis, it can put both giver and recipient in touch with the divine. Giving thanks and congratulations makes the workplace much more the way God would have it.

The opposite is equally true. The real problem with Ebenezer Scrooge was not that he didn't celebrate Christmas once a year but that he didn't give his sole employee, Bob Cratchit, the thanks and congratulations poor Bob deserved every day of the year.

Ordinary and Extraordinary

Many workplaces do practice the discipline of giving thanks and congratulations. There are many occasions when people's work is recognized, appreciated, and congratulated. People are singled out at performance review time, on birthdays, and on special days such as Administrative Professionals Day (the new term for Secretaries Day) and Bosses Day. Then there are the big occasions: twenty-fifth and fiftieth job anniversaries, promotions, and—unfortunately, in a way—retirements, transfers, and departures for other jobs.

Certainly these efforts should be honored and built on. They are what I call the "ordinary" practices of giving thanks and congratulations, and they should not be underestimated. A few years ago, the small staff at my business, in a fit of frustration at trying to come up with new, meaningful presents for each other, voted to end our tradition of having a small party over lunch for each of our birthdays. I voted for the change, but I have come to regret it, because we have lost an additional opportunity to thank and congratulate employees individually for their work—and for just being who they are. I believe that in a small way our workplace has become spiritually impoverished because of this. (I heard of one company that asks the person *having* the birthday to bring a cake or other refreshments. No gifts are expected, and it's easy to remember. Maybe my office can try this practice!)

Giving thanks and congratulations can include such simple practices as responding to notes and memos in a timely manner with a handwritten "Nice job!" or "Thanks for keeping me informed." Even the ubiquitous Post-it notes can be vehicles for letting people know that they have done a good job. People can be recognized at staff meetings for specific projects they have completed or milestones they have met. Some larger workplaces have employee newsletters or bulletin boards that document the activities and contributions of employees. In many ways, this is the easiest discipline to accomplish within the spirituality of work. All it takes is what some of the eastern spiritual masters call "mindfulness," that is, being aware of what is going on around us. In being mindful, we can remember to articulate what we are feeling toward our colleagues at work. To do this, however, we need a "trigger," some event or occurrence that reminds us to do what we already want to do. This trigger could be a birthday tickler file or an office newsletter deadline.

In addition to these ordinary practices of giving thanks and congratulations, there can be extraordinary ones, defined as such because they do not occur regularly or for everyone. These often come in the

A really cheerful, friendly person in the workplace is sometimes looked upon as being "just too nice to be true," but there is a teacher at my school who is like that and I have truly come to respect her. When I first met her, I thought she was probably insincere, but I have found that her compliments are not empty. They are sincere and specific, not a fixed set for everyone. She compliments both children and adults alike.

One of the best compliments I received from her started with "I heard something nice about you this weekend, and I just have to tell you!" I suddenly realized how nice it is to simply pass on a compliment to the one it is actually about. We've all been told when someone insults us behind our backs, but shouldn't we rather hear from people when others have been complimenting us instead?

Doreen M. Badeaux — special-education teacher, Port Arthur, Texas form of an unexpected gift to recognize a special accomplishment. This recognition is for no purpose except to give the person thanks and congratulations. This gift can be a material thing, such as flowers or candy, but it can also be something intangible, such as an extra day off or a pat on the back.

One small practice I try to follow is to let my employees leave work early. This can't happen every day, of course, and usually it's only fifteen minutes or half an hour. But on a day that's not too busy and I'm able to help cover the phones, I like to say to one of my workers, "Why don't you take off early today?" Sometimes they accept, and other times they demur, but the smile I receive when I do this always increases my spiritual capital (and never seems to hurt my economic capital either). I don't even have to say why I am making the offer. It is implied and understood that I am just thanking them for the hard work they do and recognizing that they might like to get home a few minutes early some days.

Another extraordinary idea occurred to my partner and me a few years ago when we received an offer from the Chicago Cubs to purchase fifty or more tickets to a day game

In the same way that saying "I love you" can be hollow if the actions do not jive with the words, saying "thank you" can ring hollow if we are generally unappreciative or too critical of others' efforts.

Spiritually, I think saying "thank you" tells much about our general attitude. I think it reflects an understanding on our part that in the end no one really has to do anything he or she doesn't want to do and that we are all really "coworkers" and very much interdependent on one another. From a practical standpoint, praising people when they do well or go "above and beyond" reinforces people's good work much more effectively than constantly criticizing them. Let's face it, people show up at work primarily in order to make a living, but we ultimately want to find meaning in what we do. If we feel that no one else in our workplace cares, why should we?

Joseph Pierce—noise-control specialist and community-theater actor
Syracuse, New York

at Wrigley Field in either April or September for the token price of one dollar each. We bought a hundred tickets for a game on a Tuesday afternoon in September. We then invited everyone connected with our business—from authors to freelancers to suppliers to the UPS drivers and the mail deliverer—to come to the game. We even sent tickets to our colleagues from other publishing houses. Everyone met at our building for "hot dogs and suds" at noon and then were ferried to the ballpark. We also hired someone to answer our phones for the afternoon so that we could take our entire staff. We used every ticket that year, and it established a new practice of thanks and congratulations that has grown and is anticipated by everyone connected with our business. It is truly a spiritual event, in addition to being a lot of fun.

Self-Congratulation

In addition to thanking and congratulating everyone around us, however, it may be an equally wise idea spiritually to thank and congratulate ourselves for our work. This does not often naturally occur to us. Many of us find it easy to recognize the work of others, but we are less inclined to reflect on the goodness of our own work.

Yet who knows the work we do better than we, ourselves, know it? Even the most conscientious supervisor does not have total access to the motivations, the effort, the care, and the quality that his or her employees put into their work. Many workers do not have a good supervisor or even close colleagues to give them thanks and congratulations. Take, as an obvious example, the work of a single parent. If that parent does not recognize his or her own work, who else will? Perhaps a relative or—years later—the children themselves will. But no one outside the family can possibly know the work that person does, much less think to offer a thank-you.

Even in the world of paid employment, money is not enough thanks for good work. We all need to be congratulated for what we have accomplished, and if we don't do so for ourselves, perhaps no one will.

What are some examples of the practice of self-congratulation? It might be something as simple as leaning back in a chair after a particularly good piece of work and saying to ourselves, "That was good!" or "This wouldn't have happened if not for my work." It might be having a lunch out, rather than in, or taking one of those personal or comp days that accumulate but never seem to get used. One of the ways that I reward myself for working hard is to take an hour and go to a bookstore or art gallery during working hours. This can't be done every day or even every week, of course, but I have found that to "play hooky" once every month or two does wonders for my soul—and for the quality of my work.

Compensation

None of these practices of thanks and congratulations mean much if a person is being exploited. There is nothing as hollow as an "employee appreciation" campaign in a company that hasn't offered anyone (except, in some cases, its top executives) a raise in years. The question of compensation in the workplace, then, is part of the discipline of giving thanks and congratulations. Raises, bonuses, and promotions freely given and even unexpected are wonderful ways to thank and congratulate people. It is also a matter of simple justice. "A full day's pay for a full day's work" is not a bad formula for the spirituality of work, but what that means in today's economy has changed drastically.

I cannot believe, for example, how many good, Christian employers believe that a just wage is whatever the market will bear or—even worse—whatever people are willing to accept for their work. There is

> **I try to remember** to thank people who work hard for me on projects by noting their accomplishments and contributions to their managers. Depending on the length of a project and the amount of effort expended, I also take these people to lunch. I'm not always able to do this, but I keep trying.
>
> **Teri Tanner**—information technology audit manager, Arlington, Massachusetts

no spiritual dimension to this approach. It is not going to get anyone in touch with the God who knows how to give, who is the essence of generosity. "I have come that you might have life and have it more abundantly" is how Jesus summarized his mission. It seems to me that this should describe the mission of any follower of Jesus as well. (I don't think Jesus was talking about life after death, either. He was talking about daily life, our "daily bread," which we derive in large part from our daily work.)

Does that mean that everyone should get paid the same, that capitalism doesn't work, and that companies do not have to cut costs or even terminate some employees? The power of a free-market economy to provide for the well-being of a great majority of people has been pretty well proven. Some people are more talented than others; some work harder than others; some do work that is more valuable than others' work. There is no reason that they should not be better compensated than others.

It is a big jump from that observation, however, to saying that the present economic system is without flaw. From a spiritual point of view, it cannot be true that the work of the CEOs of some companies is worth a thousand times that of some other of their employees, just as it cannot be true that because you can get people to work full time for minimum wage they are justly compensated.

> **Years ago I found** a very simple and most rewarding spiritual exercise. I decided that each time I had to address a person—be it at work, on the street, when buying something, or in any other circumstance—I would smile (from the heart, no "toothpaste" smile) while at the same time reminding myself that the person I was addressing was beloved by God.
>
> It is most rewarding. People seem to need smiles. More frequently than not, they smile back. It becomes both a contemplative prayer for me and a friendly and unpretentious human action between the two of us.
>
> **Ana-Maria Rizzuto**—medical doctor
> Brookline, Massachusetts

Some people say that paying people fairly is a matter of laws and regulations, and others insist that it is a matter of letting the economy operate on the basis of self-interest. There may be some truth to both sides of that classic argument, but I'd like to suggest that from a spiritual viewpoint the key is the discipline of giving thanks and congratulations at work. To put it another way, if we develop the spirit of giving thanks and congratulations in our workplaces, we will already be on the path to just compensation for all.

Competitors

Here is the ultimate test of the spiritual discipline of giving thanks and congratulations: Can we do so to our competitors? These competitors may be within our own workplaces—fellow employees who are competing for promotions or assignments or raises. Or our competitors may be external—businesses or agencies thatproduce or provide similar goods or services.

I enjoy competing in the marketplace as much as anyone. I like looking at my company's bottom line and seeing it grow, and I am delighted when I publish a book that succeeds. But that doesn't mean that I can't be happy when others succeed or that I can't admire them when they produce a superior product or marketing strategy. In fact, if I am smart, I learn from my competitors and am challenged by them.

Is it possible to give thanks and congratulations to one's competitors? It depends on where we are coming from spiritually. If our primary identity is our competitiveness, then it seems fairly hypocritical to recognize and glory in the accomplishments of those with whom we compete. But what if our understanding of ourselves was much deeper? What if we thought of our competitors and ourselves as first and foremost, to use Jesus' phrase, "children of God"? Wouldn't we then be willing to recognize the contributions and successes of others, our brothers and sisters if you will, even if we were in competition with them on a different level?

Sports is a good training ground for this spiritual sophistication. Certainly, most professional athletes are extremely competitive. When they are playing their game, they want nothing more than to win, even to dominate their competitors. But the more spiritually advanced athletes are able to appreciate the talents and efforts of their opponents and even congratulate them for it. Who can forget the grace of Sammy Sosa when he hugged Mark McGwire in the game in St. Louis when McGwire broke Roger Maris's single-season home-run record before Sosa did? Who does not approve of kids' teams that, win or lose, line up to thank and congratulate their opposing team? Why can't we exercise that same spirit in the workplace?

Actually, we can, but it would take some spiritual discipline. With our internal competitors, it may be a matter of a kind word or note when they do something well—even if they do it "better" than we did or "beat" us in some sort of competitive effort. Part of this practice may include reminding ourselves that the success of our colleagues also reflects well on our organization as a whole and will benefit us because we are part of the whole.

> **I think it is essential** that we express gratitude to each other in the workplace. As a director of religious education, I love getting communication from people who add a note of appreciation for my work. In return, I do the same for others when appropriate, especially for volunteer catechists and helpers. I have developed many friendships in my field of ministry because of this simple practice.
>
> My husband, on the other hand, has received very little affirmation, feedback, or support in this regard in fifteen years as a salesperson, either from customers or people he works with. Even when he has increased profits, he has gotten little recognition for his efforts.
>
> **Andrea Sabor**—parish director of religious education, diocesan consultant for catechesis, wife, mother, and grandmother
> Green Bay, Wisconsin

With outside competitors, it may be a little more difficult to express our thanks and congratulations. We may not even know them personally, and any show of recognition might be viewed as insincere or worse. Still, many of us do know our competitors. We run into them in professional associations, in trade organizations, even in the marketplace as we compete with them. Sometimes the practice of

I have started thanking the heretofore unthanked preparers of the student suppers that we host by introducing and requesting applause for the cooks in the middle of our rather loud gatherings. It takes about two seconds, but it adds a note of thanks and makes the often rushed meals more grace filled.

Thomas Holahan, CSP—Catholic priest, campus minister, and member of a religious community, Boulder, Colorado

---

For me, the most important recognition of work done well is the recognition I give myself for my self-motivation to get it done. I am gifted to work with two other people who are also self-motivated. We take pride in what we do and don't rely upon each other for thanks or congratulations.

Once in a while, we mark some special occasion (never the same one) in some spontaneous way—usually lunch together. We do make it a point to tell each other when we think the other has done a good job on a project, but to do that too often would lessen the meaning. In other words, we keep celebration for the really special occasions and take personal pride in our daily work.

Mark G. Boyer—Catholic priest, newspaper editor, and author Springfield, Missouri

giving thanks and congratulations might just require that we have a friendly attitude. Sometimes it may mean formal recognition of the other person's accomplishment or success.

At the bare minimum, I think, this discipline would mean that we not bad-mouth our competitors, spread false information about them, resort to negative advertising against them, or engage in any unfair marketing practices. This may seem obvious to those trying to live a Christian spiritual life, but it is amazing how many of us don't make this connection when we take our faith to work.

By the way, when we give thanks and congratulations to ourselves and to others for work, it is not a huge step to occasionally remember to give thanks to God as well. We Christians call ourselves a eucharistic people. *Eucharist* means "thanksgiving." How we give that thanks to God may fall more into the traditional realm of religion—prayer, liturgy, ritual—but it would also have to be part of any spirituality of work.

Practicing the Discipline

- List five ordinary ways that you give thanks and congratulations to others at work. Put the list somewhere where you will notice it each day. Each time you do any of the practices, try to be more aware of their connection with the transcendent nature of God.

- Think of someone in your workplace who deserves recognition that he or she has not received lately. Think of an unexpected, extraordinary way you could give that person thanks and congratulations—and then do it. Mark on your calendar to do a similar thing for someone else in your workplace each month or quarter.

- Once a week, remember to thank yourself for your good work. Develop little rewards that you give yourself—a lunch out, getting to work late or leaving early, or buying yourself a specific gift.

- Once a year, review whether or not you feel you are justly paid. If not, then do something about it (ask for a raise). If you are justly paid, look around for someone who may not be and try to do something about it (give them a raise or encourage them to ask for one).

- Find a competitor each month to whom you can pay a compliment or about whom you can say something nice, and then do it. Make note of the reactions you receive.

- Develop your own prayer of thanksgiving to God for your work and the work of others. Decide on a regular time when you will say it—each day before you begin work, each week at Sunday services, or as part of your daily prayer.

Chapter 7

Building Support and Community

The best possible work has not yet been done.

Margaret Mead

For many people, the workplace experience is anything but spiritual. They find it full of competition, jealousy, gossip, backstabbing, pressure, and tension—nothing like the way God would have it. Practitioners of the spirituality of work, however, can transform their daily environment by helping to build support and community in the workplace.

This discipline is closely related to the discipline of giving thanks and congratulations in the workplace. In fact, building support and community at work is a direct result of giving thanks and congratulations. But the pace of the typical business day and the demands of the market economy militate against spending the time and effort necessary to build relationships and to be supportive of others.

Still, it can be done—even in the most hostile of work environments. But real community happens only when we work at it consciously and conscientiously over a long period of time. Here are some specific practices that will contribute to the kind of community building that is truly spiritual.

Offering Welcome

Most workplaces today have something of a revolving-door feel. Colleagues, supervisors, employees, customers, suppliers, freelancers, temporary and part-time workers come and go. I have taken new jobs several times in my career, so I have experienced being the "new kid on the block." If I was blessed, I found someone in my new workplace who instinctively practiced the discipline of building support and community.

We all know this person. Perhaps he or she introduced us around to others when we started a new job, stopped by several times to see how we were doing, invited us out to lunch, explained the ins and outs of life at our new workplace, even told us where the "dead bodies" were buried or what buttons we needed to avoid pushing. The welcomer may not have become our best friend at work. We may have found we had much more in common with others. Still, he or she continued to have a nice word for us and made sure that we felt invited to participate in group activities.

After we had been there awhile, we began to notice that this same person not only made new people feel welcome but also made sure that the people who had been there longer did not feel threatened. The welcomer encouraged everyone to feel part of a team, allowing no one to become isolated and discouraging or subverting cliques through his or her community-building efforts.

We too can practice the discipline of welcoming. It is mostly an awareness of the needs of others and a willingness to break through our shy tendencies and away from the social habits of leaving people alone. If people don't want to be welcomed, they will let us know pretty quickly. But most people are eager for a friendly word or gesture, especially in a new workplace.

My business often deals with its customers on the telephone. We spend a lot of time training our staff to welcome customers, some of whom may be upset, nervous, or outright belligerent. Certainly, there is an ulterior motive to this—we want happy customers who think well of us and who will return with more business. Our welcoming, however, is also done for its own sake. It's just a better way to be, and it provides a better environment to work in. When we are welcoming to others, we often find that they reciprocate, which makes our own work experience all the more holy and satisfying.

> **The discipline of** recognizing the good done by coworkers, the grace evident in particular transactions, the value of systems and procedures that promote the best in us, and the benefits our work is providing to the wider human community can reinforce our attempts to be "kingdom of God" people at work. Fortunately, this discipline is also good management practice.
>
> The discipline of searching for the spirituality in troublesome situations and trying relationships can be more difficult. It requires the gift of community—both in the workplace and within our faith communities.
>
> **James L. Nolan**—lawyer and business-conference director, husband, father, and grandfather, Washington, D.C.

Being Loyal

If there is one main thing that people today feel they have lost in the contemporary workplace, it is any sense of loyalty. Companies are not loyal to their workers; employees are not loyal to their employers; and workers are not loyal to each other. This loss is described by all parties with regret and a sense of inevitability.

Into this situation comes the practitioner of the spirituality of work. It would be naive to think that the sense of loyalty in the workplace that existed in the past could ever be completely restored. The current global economy will probably not allow it. Still, small steps can be taken—steps that may begin to reintroduce loyalty into a particular workplace. Gossiping and backbiting are examples of a good place to start. Isn't it a sign of disloyalty to tear down others? Doesn't that serve to destroy community in the workplace? The fact that "everyone does it" makes it only more imperative that those seeking to incarnate the spirit of God in the workplace do the opposite. Perhaps one discipline we could practice would be to walk out of the room when people begin putting others down or—better yet—to talk positively about those being slandered or calumniated.

> **My only workaday** spiritual discipline is this: whenever I find myself silently cursing something or someone (including, especially, myself), I try to come up with a blessing to bestow as well. So "damn" copiers and "idiot" clients and my "foolish" self get a blessing that supersedes the curse.
>
> **Joseph S. Moore**—financial-software consultant, husband, and father
> Concord, California

Another example of building loyalty in the workplace might be backing people up rather than secretly (or not so secretly) reveling in their difficulties. If someone has made a mistake or failed at some project, perhaps we could offer a word of encouragement or a reminder of that person's good effort, rather than joining in the criticism or silent treatment he or she is receiving.

Even loyalty to the company or the employer—undeserved or unreciprocated as it might be—could be a spiritual practice. "A full day's work for a full day's pay" is still a pretty good goal. Cheating, bad-mouthing, and stealing from a "disloyal" employer may feel good at the time, but doesn't it bring employees down—spiritually speaking—to that same level? Likewise, if a company constantly undermines or threatens the security of its employees, doesn't it produce the very disloyalty it complains about? What if the employer or employee went first and actually exhibited loyalty—with no guarantee or even hope that it would be returned? Might not this begin to build support and community in the workplace? And might not this potentially unrequited loyalty be considered a spiritual— as well as a courageous—act?

Perhaps loyalty in the workplace can be practiced only in tiny baby steps before it can return to the level it once had in our economic life. If so, isn't it time we got started?

Showing Compassion

Perhaps there is no place where the public life of work

> **When some of us** were offered an optional early retirement package from our employer, we formed a group for mutual support and community. We met weekly, first to decide whether to take the package, then to help each other understand and make use of the career counseling and benefits being offered.
>
> When we first started meeting, we were all pretty angry, but we managed to turn it around. We shook up our employer by refusing the offer of individual retirement parties and insisted on having one large group party. But the highlight of our festivities clearly was our leave-taking ceremony on our last day. We wanted to pray together before we left and invited our friends that were remaining to join us. Then all of us "downsized" employees left together in decorated cars and met at a pub to celebrate. By the time we finished, all of our anger was gone. The power of the group and the power of prayer had taken care of it. It was amazing!
>
> **Kathy Hills**—university project administrator, wife, and mother, Chicago, Illinois

Accepting the Resurrection requires a conviction that things can change and be transformed, including the workplace. That underlying philosophy is what led me to develop the nontraditional admissions process that we use at our college to admit adult students. We don't make our decisions based on transcripts or test scores that may be a decade or more old and may only describe who the student was then. Because we believe that people can change, we make our admissions decisions based on how well the student does in his or her first four courses here with us.

I can't tell you how relieved many adults feel about that. Often their early grades from another college had more to say about the fact that they were in school only because their parents wanted them to be there or that they were away from home for the first time. They are worried that their "permanent record" will eliminate them from going back to college. These are folks who have already gone on to establish themselves in their workplaces. They have internal motivation to complete a degree and are thrilled that they can get another chance at a challenging institution. Many of them do extremely well, partly because of the sense of support and community we try to build among our adult student body, our faculty, and our alumni.

Hilary Ward Schnadt—university administrator, wife, Chicago, Illinois

and the private life of an employee intersect more abruptly than at times of sadness, loss, or personal difficulty. A death or serious illness, family problems, depression, addiction—none of these tragedies can be neatly segregated from the workplace. How we deal with these situations, however, is a sure sign of our spiritual depth and sophistication.

Sometimes a tragedy is obvious—a sudden death or sickness, for example. In these cases, coworkers will often come together to offer sympathy or help, going out of their way to visit a hospital or attend a wake or funeral, offering a listening ear or a shoulder to cry on. Workplace policies are often quite liberal in these cases, providing employees with paid leave to deal with a situation. Many will testify how important such support in the workplace can be.

In other workplaces, however, employers and colleagues can be much less sympathetic. Some maintain that personal problems should not intrude into the workplace at all. They feel that work is where people get on with their lives and that the workplace is ill equipped to deal with people's personal concerns.

In some cases, people's situations are not obvious or are well hidden. While prying into the personal lives of colleagues is certainly not appropriate, an atmosphere where openness to and understanding of personal problems is encouraged can be created in the workplace. Sometimes things come to light because the quality of performance at work is affected. Other times, a person will share what is going on with a close colleague or supervisor, who must then decide whether and how to let others in the workplace know.

> **I believe that** the discipline of building support and community in the workplace comes from a fundamental belief that all of us have an equal right to human dignity—whether one is the janitor or the CEO. Once we truly accept this notion and integrate it into our lives, treating employees, clients, and even our competitors with respect becomes a spiritual engagement.
>
> For example, there is a tendency for employees—and particularly supervisors—to breeze by the receptionist with a quick "hello" at best. On the other hand, the expenditure of five seconds for a sincere "how are things going" and another ten seconds to truly listen to the response can become a spiritual act.
>
> **William H. Farley**—commercial real estate developer, husband, father, and grandfather Hartford, Connecticut

In the midst of these situations, we can practice the discipline of building support and community in the workplace in a variety of ways. How we respond personally, how we involve others, how we set and enforce (or make exceptions to) personnel policies—all have real effect. They put us and others in our workplace in touch with the "ultimately meaningful" in our lives.

Personally, I hate the fact that we even have to have policies in my company for being compassionate. Who are we to say that somebody can have so many days off for this tragedy or that sickness in his or her life? How are we to decide how much money we should give to this

When I made the decision to go back to graduate school as a middle-aged single mother, I could have gone to law or business school and I would probably be richer financially now. But I chose to get a degree in education and to teach writing because it fit my talents better. I chose to take a position at a state university rather than a religious institution because I feel it gives me a way to live my Christian witness through my work.

One of the reasons I wanted to be a college instructor is because I thought this work would allow me to spend the time and effort necessary to build relationships and be supportive of others in the workplace. I have found that I can build a sense of community among my students by making my classes fun and trying to be available to my students without invading their privacy.

Sharon E. Strand—college instructor, faculty advisor, mother, and grandmother Spearfish, South Dakota

or that good cause? But, of course, we must have these policies or we couldn't operate. In fact, most people want to know what they can expect in the workplace when it comes to compassion. Very few want to milk a situation or receive undo consideration.

The issue is not whether we should have policies, but rather what the policies are and how flexible they might be. For example, my company has a policy that an employee gets three days of paid leave for a death in the family. Recently, the elderly grandmother of one of our part-time secretaries died after a long illness. Our policy seemed perfectly compassionate to both my secretary and to me. But what if her grandmother had died suddenly or tragically or in a faraway state? What if our secretary had been especially close to her grandmother and took the death especially hard? Then—using the "do unto others" principle—I hope that we would have been flexible and compassionate enough to work out some extra time for our secretary so that she could grieve without being financially penalized.

Some people might take advantage of such generosity. But whose problem—spiritually, at least—is that? And for every one that does take advantage of our compassion, how many wouldn't dream of it—

ten, twenty, a hundred? Would we take advantage? If we would, perhaps most others will too. But if we wouldn't do it, why are we so worried about lots of other people doing so?

Often we really don't know how best to show compassion in the workplace. Part of the reason, I think, is that we tend to separate our personal and work lives, and some of that is healthy. We cannot be as emotionally involved with people in the workplace as we are with our own families and close friends. Yet the opposite is also true. We cannot treat coworkers as if they have no feelings, problems, or personal lives. We must be able to offer them an appropriate measure of compassion as the need arises if we are to build workplaces of support and community.

Having Fun

"All work and no play makes Jack a dull boy" is a saying with which the practitioners of a spirituality of work concur. The discipline of building support and community includes introducing some fun and joy into the workaday world.

Some people do it with simply a smile; others tell jokes or regularly kid around with colleagues and customers. A few people have a talent for organizing parties, dinners, and after-work excursions. They are the ones behind the company softball team, bowling league, sports pools, newsletters, and other fun activities. One woman I know has a contest in her

If we are not having fun at work then we are not legitimately "the subject of work," as Pope John Paul II put it. Nor are others we work with or the people we serve. There is no community that is sustainable if there is no fun. Part of this fun, however, will be based on the tough times when we work as a community in our workplaces, developing the stories and myths that through time become the foundation of the culture of our organizations.

Thomas A. Bausch—professor of management, husband, father, and grandfather Milwaukee, Wisconsin workplace for "best cartoon of the week," which is then posted beside the watercooler.

When I take a call from a customer at my business, the caller almost always starts by saying, "I'd like to place an order." I try to get a laugh with some response such as "Good, that's why we're in business" or "Great, you just made my day." I feel that if I can make a customer laugh, we are both somehow a little closer to the kingdom of God.

Management philosophy and policy can encourage or discourage fun in the workplace, so part of the spirituality of work is to make sure that owners and managers see the benefits of a happy work environment. Thus does the discipline of building support and community in the workplace institutionalize itself.

Redefining "Evangelization"

A lot of religious professionals think that the spirituality of work is (or should be) about what they call "evangelization." They think that the purpose of spiritual practices in the workplace is to get yourself noticed and then to convert others or proselytize them to join your particular sect or denomination. For the most part, this strategy only succeeds in giving spirituality, or at least religion, a bad name in the work environment.

The spirituality of work is about evangelization, but not by means of proselytizing or in the fundamentalist understanding of the term. For Christians, spirituality is about getting in tune with God as revealed by Jesus of Nazareth and then working to bring about God's kingdom "on earth as it is in heaven." Building support and community in the workplace is part of that ongoing task.

This kind of evangelization is more about actions than about words. It does not need to clothe itself in religious language to be effective—in fact, it is usually more effective if it is put in the shared, common language of today's pluralistic workplace. Engaging in pious practices—reading the Bible, praying, visiting a church—may well help your spiritual life, but as Jesus recommended they are better done behind closed doors. The disciplines of the spirituality of work, however, can be practiced without pushing our religious beliefs on anyone. In fact, they can be done without any references to religion at all. By our fruits they will know us, Jesus promised.

Does this mean that we are ashamed or embarrassed by our religious faith? Of course not. In fact, if we consistently practice the disciplines suggested in this book, I suspect we will stand out like a sore thumb in most workplaces. Our practice of the spirituality of work may well open up many conversations with others in the workplace about where we are coming from and what our religious motivation might be. And in those conversations people may well discover that they would like to share the kind of religious faith and affiliation we enjoy.

But this cannot be our starting point. Our purpose for practicing the disciplines of the spirituality of work must not be to convert others to our way of thinking but to convert ourselves to a better work life. Once we have done that, evangelization will take care of itself.

Practicing the Discipline

- Go out of your way each week to welcome the newest person in your workplace with a "random act of kindness." Do the same for one of the existing workers who may be feeling threatened or isolated.

- Every time someone starts backbiting or gossiping, point out a good thing about the person being criticized. If the conversation continues, walk out of the room.

- Once a week, encourage one person who has made a mistake or failed at something. Remind the person of the good work he or she has done. Or do something special for someone who is hurting in your workplace.

- Review your workplace's family illness or bereavement policies. Try to change the policies, if needed.

- Try to inject a bit of levity into every workday. Organize or help with a fun activity in your workplace.

- If you've been proselytizing in the workplace, stop. But if someone asks about your spiritual beliefs, offer to take them to lunch and talk about it.

Chapter 8

Dealing with Others As You Would Have Them Deal with You

It is no use walking anywhere to preach unless our walking is our preaching.

Francis of Assisi

The Golden Rule. Sure, sure, I'll try to treat others as I'd like to be treated. Within reason, of course. I mean, the workplace is a jungle, isn't it? I can't be expected to change the corporate culture all by myself, can I? If I don't follow the rules, I'll be eaten up, won't I?

At best, many people—including Christians—view the basic injunction of Jesus to "love your neighbor as yourself" as a prescription to "be nice." Holding the door open for others, issuing a cheery "have a nice day," remembering a coworker's birthday or anniversary—these are often the limit of the kinds of actions we think of when we consider love in the workplace.

In and of themselves, these are positive things, maybe the sine qua non starting place for humanizing the work environment. Certainly, anyone who has been in a job where basic civility was not the norm can attest to its value and necessity. Haven't we all encountered a rude salesperson, a surly truck driver, an aloof secretary, or a demanding boss and wondered why he or she couldn't just treat others as human beings? And we have probably all had days when we wouldn't have wanted to deal with ourselves!

So, being nice in the workplace is not a bad thing. In fact, giving thanks and congratulations and building support and community in the workplace may be among the first steps in practicing the spirituality of work. But these are not the last, the only, or even the most important steps. Of all the disciplines of the spirituality of work, the practice of dealing with others as we would have them deal with us on a regular and comprehensive basis in our workplaces would effect the most radical, challenging, and difference-making change in how we go about our work.

Honesty

If we really had it our way, how honest would we want others in the workplace to be with us? The answer is pretty darn honest. I'm not talking about an unhealthy scrupulosity here. (That can be a sin.) No one cares if someone exaggerates a little about their product or service ("the best-tasting pizza on the South Side") or tells a little white lie ("Thank you for your complaint. We appreciate it"). But there are serious, systematic situations in the workplace where the truth is ignored or viewed at best as an inconvenience. "Everybody is doing it" is the usual justification, but the spirituality of work does not tolerate that excuse.

Let's take a simple and obvious example: being under-charged. It happens all the time—in supermarkets, in restaurants, in deliveries, and in the workplace. How do most of us want to be dealt with if we are the ones who are doing the undercharging? Obviously, we are grateful— sometimes, unfortunately, even surprised—when the other person points out our mistake: "You only charged me for fifty of these, but you sent a hundred." We are delighted. We thank the person profusely and then readjust the bill and breathe a big sigh of relief.

I have spent a lifetime in the often rough-and-tumble world of commercial real estate. I have tried to practice the Golden Rule at all times and have been generally rewarded with great response from customer, client, and competitor. Lest you think that I am a Pollyanna, there have been times when the reciprocal action has not been as pure as I'd have liked, but I believe that it has been great more than 95 percent of the time. So I still try very hard to do unto others as I hope and pray they do unto me.

William H. Farley—commercial real estate developer, husband, father, and grandfather Hartford, Connecticut

But what happens when it goes the other way? Do we quietly pocket the difference, feeling that we have gotten something for nothing and perhaps blaming the other person for being incompetent? Sometimes, we even justify not saying anything because we feel that all mistakes even out eventually.

If we apply the discipline of dealing with others as we would have them deal with us, however, our course would be clear. We would notify the other party of their mistake and willingly pay the fair amount. It would be automatic. There wouldn't even be anything to

My family was looking for a hotel for one night. We got to a particular economy hotel, but my wife was reluctant because of the cheap price—she prefers chain hotels, although she always chooses the cheapest of the chains. But we decided to give this one a try, and the night's stay was fine.

What was remarkable to me was the quality care given by the owner as he checked each person in to the hotel. Judging from their dress and vehicles, several other customers were from the lower levels of the economic ladder. But while we all waited in an extended line outside a bulletproof glass window, the owner took time and care with each person—calling each by name; talking to each child; giving clear, simple instructions; and efficiently processing the necessary data.

I thought to myself that this innkeeper was dealing with us as he would want us to deal with him—offering inexpensive lodging to poor, tired travelers, treating us with respect and hospitality when we arrived.

Love in this context has a texture that can be experienced and appreciated. What if all business people acted this way? What a different world it would be. It saddens me to realize that the gulf between reality and the kingdom of God is so large.

Michael Galligan-Stierle—director of campus ministry, husband, and father
Wheeling, West Virginia

think about. My father used to run a grocery store, and he had a policy of checking each and every delivery very carefully. When something was missing, he was quick to demand that it be corrected. But when he received an overshipment, he was just as quick to notify the supplier. Maybe this practice seems obvious to you and you wouldn't think about operating any other way. If so, congratulations and keep it up! It is not how everyone in the marketplace acts. (You can tell just by the way people react when you do it. Their surprise makes you wonder what they do when the same thing happens to them.)

If we take this Golden Rule approach a little further, however, it gets a little trickier. Take this scenario: we order something and it comes a little flawed or there is a mistake in the order. We have done nothing wrong; it is clearly the fault of the supplier. We can easily and justifiably refuse the product or use the mistake to pressure the supplier into giving us a big discount on the defective or overrun material. Here again is where this discipline of the spirituality of work kicks in. If the situation were reversed, how would we hope to be treated? Are we willing to treat the other person in that way? Therein, I submit, is a path to holiness.

This question of honesty in the workplace is multifaceted. Are we advertising truthfully, the way we would like others to advertise? Are we evaluating others the way we would want to be evaluated? Do we tell the truth to our customers or clients when we are wrong? Do we bill fairly and accurately? Are we honest with employees and stockholders about profitability, plans for the future, management changes, product quality, and so forth?

The question that the spirituality of work always raises is "What if?" What if we were honest about all of these things? What kind of workers would we be, and what kind of workplaces would we have?

> **The greatest gift** an employer or manager can give is an honest and open evaluation of our work. It should be done in a caring manner and with an effort to coach us into improving our performance, but it must be honest. Just as my collegiate coaches wanted to help me be the best athlete that I could be, so my business "coaches" wanted to help me be the best businessperson I could be.
>
> There should be no sweet talk and no avoidance in these performance reviews but only an honest and caring evaluation of our work. For many supervisors this is a frightening thing to do, but that's where the discipline of dealing with others as we would have them deal with us comes in. We owe it to those who work for us.
>
> **William A. Diehl**—business consultant and writer, husband, father, and grandfather Allentown, Pennsylvania

Customer Service

Customer relations/client services is another big area in which to test this discipline of dealing with others as you would have them deal with you. Almost all of us have been treated shabbily in the marketplace, and we know how negatively we react. We have also been treated wonderfully and have appreciated that.

I once found a monthly charge on one of my credit cards for twelve dollars. When I called to inquire about it, I was told that it was for credit card protection. This was a service I had never ordered. Unfortunately, I had not caught this charge on my statement for several months. When I tried to argue that I had never requested this service, I was hung up on (twice), ignored, insulted, told that I was wrong and that I "must have" ordered the service, and informed that there was nothing that the company could or would do. I felt angry, frustrated, and powerless. Like most people caught in that situation, I yelled and screamed, threatened legal and direct action, and in general had a very unholy and unspiritual experience. Until, that is, I finally reached a certain customer service representative, whom I nominate as a candidate for the patron saint of the spirituality of work.

This man was the first person to treat me like a human being throughout this ordeal. He was always calm, cheerful, helpful, and honest. Early on, he said the words that I wanted to hear: "I believe you, Mr. Pierce, when you say that you did not order this service." Because—through my own fault—I had waited so long before complaining, he had to fight to get the charges refunded, going on my word only. "It took an act of Congress," he told me, but he did it.

Simone Weil once said, "On the one hand, love everything without distinction. On the other, love only the good. A mystery." How this mystery works in the workplace has to be a play-by-play—really a person-by-person—solution, but the tension between trying to get beyond good and evil and living in its midst is definitely one of the challenges of being a Christian in the marketplace. We certainly can't choose one option (love without distinction) or the other (love only the good) to the exclusion of the other without missing the point of what we're doing there.

Maryanne Hannan—teacher and writer, wife, mother, and grandmother
Troy, New York

This person treated me as I wanted to be treated, and now it is incumbent upon me to treat my own customers the same way. Incumbent, that is, if I want to live the spirituality of my work. "The customer is always right" is not always true. Ask anyone in business. Christians are not called to be naive doormats in the workplace. But we are called to deal with others as we would have others deal with us.

Our customers, clients, and colleagues should be able to expect from us competency, quality, honesty, trust, service, and understanding, and we need to discipline ourselves to provide those qualities.

Negotiation

The problem with most negotiation is that it is thought of as a test between two parties in which each side attempts to negotiate the best deal for itself. This sets it up as a situation in which we win or lose, depending on our skills as negotiators. This, in turn, usually prevents either side from being generous, since we fear that the other side will take advantage of our generosity without giving anything back.

I own a small business and have had two different partners. One I eventually bought out, and the other I sold half the business to. In addition, I own a building with two other parties. In my negotiations with all of these various partners, I started by asking myself how generous I could

> **When others don't treat us** as we try to treat them, this is when the rubber hits the road. I have experienced this on my job in a law office recently. It is easy to love those who love us. When they don't, generally or specifically, then the gospel becomes a real challenge. As much as I might desire community in the workplace, the reality is often far from that. However, that doesn't excuse my continuing to try to be Christian, no matter what. The spirituality of work is just that: spirituality. It can't be achieved on a purely human or warm fuzzy level.
>
> **Dorothy Dunbar, FSPA**—law office support staff and member of a religious community Chicago, Illinois

afford to be and used that as my starting point. The reaction was mostly what I had hoped. Because my partners perceived that I was not trying to wring every dime and concession from them, all of them were willing and able to be generous with me. The negotiations proceeded rapidly, with a minimum of time and tension. (In fact, in every case the only serious problems arose when we needed to put our agreements into legal documents and the lawyers made the negotiations more adversarial than they had been up to that point.)

If we are generous in negotiations, does that mean we will be taken advantage of? Perhaps, but not necessarily. Remember: we are the ones who determine how generous we can afford to be. If we are truly being taken advantage of in a negotiation, we can always terminate the deal.

On the other hand, generosity is, by definition, not always reciprocal. My children have taught me this. They are still preteens, and their concern is whether or not things are "fair." "It's not fair," they'll say, "that you took one of us out to McDonald's and not the other two." My response has always been "Do you want me to be fair or generous? Because they are not the same thing." Initially, all three of them came down heavily on "fair," but in the last few years they have begun to see the decided advantage of having a father who is "generous" rather than "fair." (If you want to get theological about it for a moment, would we rather have a God who is fair or one who is generous? I think Jesus answered that question fairly clearly when he described God as the Father who gives only good things to his children.)

In the workplace, generosity in negotiation may not be reciprocated in every case. That, of course, takes nothing away from the spirituality of our own generosity. On the other hand, our generosity can make it possible for others to exercise generosity of their own. When that happens, the workplace does begin to be truly transformed.

Competition

Negotiation with employees and partners is one thing, but how do we deal with our competitors as we would have them deal with us? Here is the story of how one competitor did it.

In January 1984, a fire totally destroyed the Allen-Edmonds shoe factory in Belgium, Wisconsin. It looked as though the 250 employees of that firm would permanently lose their jobs, spelling economic disaster for the small town. Instead, Allen-Edmonds's president, John Stollenwerk, was able to run a pun in the newspaper within a couple of days: "We'll be back on your feet in no time."

What made Stollenwerk's advertisement possible was an act of generosity from his competitor, Robert Laverenz of Laverenz Shoe Company in nearby Sheboygan, Wisconsin. "It wasn't a question of should we or shouldn't we help out," said Laverenz. "The question was how soon and how much could we help."

Laverenz huddled with members of Local 796 of the United Food and Commercial Workers, the union for his employees. They called a meeting of their fellow workers at Laverenz Shoe Company and voted to switch to a four-day work week. "Every single hand went up in affirmation," Laverenz said in praise. When Laverenz Shoe Company closed at 4:30 on Thursday afternoons, the Allen-Edmonds employees arrived on a bus. They produced twelve

> **The gospel message** is unconditional love, unconditional trust, unconditional Jesus Christ. You go out on a limb, you trust people, and no matter how many times they slap you in the face or backstab you, you turn the other cheek. Christianity is not a "this for that" calling. It has to start somewhere, and that somewhere is among those of us who decide to take a deep breath and jump off the "cliff" of uncertainty. Some of us will undoubtedly get smacked on the rocks, but that's what being Christian is all about.
>
> **Richard P. Bohan**—educator, husband, and father, Des Plaines, Illinois

There is a price to being a Christian, and part of that price is that you will not be as successful in the ways of the world as those who appear to be moral but who are in fact uninhibited by any scruples. If they are good at it, you may never catch them in their lies, and even if you do, there is always someone else for them to deceive.

As Christians, I hope we do not behave well because we expect material reward to result. Christ behaved well, and look what he got. We should behave well in the workplace and trust that God will not give us more than we can endure. That is all we can pray for.

Joseph S. Moore—financial-software consultant, husband, and father
Concord, California

hundred pairs of shoes a week for their company by working continuous shifts through the weekends.

The sequel to this story is that today the Allen-Edmonds company is one of the few remaining manufacturers of shoes in this country. More sobering is the fact that Laverenz Shoe Company has gone out of business—not because of the assistance it gave to Allen-Edmonds but because of the competitiveness of the international shoe industry itself.

In today's marketplace, dog-eat-dog competition is the norm and is even held up as a virtue. But is it a particularly spiritual path? What does such a way of doing business do—not only to our competitors but to us? Is there an alternative way of doing business? Of course there is, and the spirituality of work will show us the way. If we could practice the discipline of dealing with our competitors as we would have them deal with us, how would we operate in the workplace?

First of all, we would eschew all unfair (and even ungenerous) business practices, even if they are legal. We would never flood a market with underpriced goods in order to drive a competitor out of business. We wouldn't consider negative advertising of our competitor's products. We wouldn't start rumors (even true ones) about our competitors to harm them. We wouldn't pay bribes (even "legal" ones) to get an unfair advantage. In other words, and very simply, we would deal with our competitors as we would have our competitors deal with us.

Does this mean that competition is not good for the economy or that practitioners of a spirituality of work cannot be successfully competitive? I do not think so, and I can point to countless examples of companies that succeed without trashing their competition. They do so by producing superior products, by providing excellent service, by advertising creatively and truthfully, and by attracting and retaining the best employees.

Just Compensation

I belong to a group of businesspeople in Chicago called Business Executives for Economic Justice (BEEJ). We meet monthly to discuss difficult issues faced by business and professional managers who are in decision-making positions in their companies and firms. We recently spent an entire year exploring the issue of just compensation. It is an issue that clarifies the question of how to deal with others as you would have them deal with you.

The market is very clear on the issue of compensation: if you pay the going rate or a little more, then you are paying a just wage. In fact, if you pay employees much more than the market rate for wages and benefits, you may be harming not only your own company but the industry as well. Another assumption is that every employee must be treated exactly alike in terms of compensation and benefits, despite their personal or family circumstances.

While there is not a starry-eyed liberal in the group, the members of BEEJ struggled mightily with this issue, for most of us realized that the present system of compensation in this country—and worldwide for that matter—is not just. We did not come up with any easy answers, but our guiding principle was to ask ourselves how we would want to be dealt with when it came to compensation for our work and then to apply that to others.

How about in your own personal situation, whether you are an employer, a manager, or an employee? Do you feel that everyone is being compensated as you yourself would want to be compensated?

What would happen if you started practicing that discipline? (For those of us in the church, wouldn't we have to radically reassess what we are paying our ministers and teachers?) And what would be the result of such thinking and acting? Would all of our companies and institutions go out of business? Perhaps, although no one is suggesting that changes in compensation be done overnight. But perhaps the workplace would become a more just, a more happy, and a more holy place if we dealt with others on compensation issues as we would have them deal with us.

These are but a few examples of the discipline of dealing with others in the workplace as we would like to have them deal with us. My examples may seem unrealistic. It may be impossible to imagine practicing this discipline on a regular basis. Our economic system, which is based on the assumption that people will operate in what appears to be their immediate and narrow self-interest, may not tolerate it. Still, isn't it in our self-interest to have others treat us the way we want to be treated? Maybe we have to go first. After all, Jesus didn't say, "Love others to the extent that they love you." He said, "Love others as you love yourself."

Practicing the Discipline

- Make an examination of conscience at the same time each day that includes reflecting on how you have treated others the day before and how you plan to treat others the next day.

- Take a moment before each encounter with others to decide how you hope to be treated. (One spiritual practice that has been revived and become very popular is to ask, "What would Jesus do?" A variation might be to ask yourself, "How would I deal with Jesus, and how would I want Jesus to deal with me?")

- If you have a close friend, spouse, or colleague who is on the same spiritual page, role-play how you plan to handle a particular situation with someone in your workplace. If no one is available, role-play the situation in your own mind. First, take the role of the other person and imagine how he or she will react to you. Then think about how you might react to him or her. Go back and forth with this, developing several scenarios, all based on your acting toward the other as you would want that person to act toward you. After the actual encounter, spend five minutes reviewing what happened, what you did well, and what you wish you had done differently.

• Spend a few moments each day keeping an ongoing list. On one side list "Times I Did unto Others" and on the other side list "Times Others Did unto Me." Keep track only of the times you treated others as you would like to be treated or others treated you that way. Observe which list is longer.

Chapter 9

Deciding What Is "Enough"—and Sticking to It

If one has to establish communion with God through
some means, why not through the spinning wheel?

Mahatma Gandhi

In Chicago's Goodman Theater production of *A Christmas Carol,* one of the characters says wistfully, *"Enough,* what a glorious word." And when Jesus asked the disciples what they had to feed the multitude and they said five loaves and two fishes, he said, basically, "That is enough."

Deciding what is "enough" in the workplace and then sticking to it is a very underrated virtue. How much of the pressure, the busyness, the competition, the unhappiness, and the inability to see God in our work results from our failure to practice this discipline? For example, we get people working on an assembly line or another repetitive job, and then we establish goals for productivity. The workers finally meet those goals but then find that it is not enough, that the standards have been raised. A person opens a retail store, hoping that sales might reach half a million dollars some day. That goal is met, but it is no longer enough. A lawyer or accountant puts in extra hours on a big case, only to find three more similar jobs added to his or her load.

It seems that in the workplace enough is never enough. Whether it is time, money, energy, or attention, we do not have the ability to say no. That is where this discipline of the spirituality of work comes in. We must build into our workday ways of reminding ourselves of what is enough and strategies for sticking to our decisions.

But how can we practice this discipline, especially in a society and a workplace that seem intent on convincing us that we need more of everything and that it is virtually impossible to have enough? And if we cannot find a way, will we ever really get in touch with the God of plenty in our work?

Enough Money

Let's tackle the toughest question first: What is enough when it comes to money or material goods? The old joke is that it is "just a little bit more than I've got," or better yet, "just a little bit more than my neighbor has." This idea, which does seem to be the functioning definition for many of us, is spiritually bankrupt, for it dooms us from ever being truly satisfied. As D. H. Lawrence wrote:

The wages of work is cash.
The wages of cash is want more cash.
The wages of want more cash is vicious competition.
The wages of vicious competition is—the world we live in.

Voluntary poverty, the idea at the other end of the philosophical spectrum, also seems to be a nonanswer for most people. First of all, it is unrealistic. It is obvious that not everyone is going to choose poverty, so if we build a spirituality that demands it, we have by definition created a spirituality for the few. Second, it is not clear that an economy based on poverty for all is what the God of abundance has in mind for us. If we are all poor, who cares for the poor?

So how do we decide when we have enough material goods? For most of us, one simple discipline is to admit that we already have enough.

> **I had always aspired** for more authority, responsibility, and recognition on the job. When I joined my current company, it was with a quite different purpose. I had decided that what I truly enjoyed most was hands-on project work, and my new employer offered the opportunity to say "Enough!" to the demands of continually searching for advancement.
>
> In return, I am more at peace with myself in my work environment than I have been in a long time, and that peace has carried over into my family life as well. I believe that we are at our best when we know our real abilities and limitations, and being able to say "Enough already!" without regret or second guesses is a big step toward getting there.
>
> **Daniel Minarik**—engineer, husband, father, and grandfather, Buffalo Grove, Illinois

Not that there aren't some things we want or even need; not that we are going to stop striving for more; and not that we have to accept unjust payment or the abuse of our talents. This discipline would be simply a matter of reminding ourselves regularly that we have been blessed with whatever material possessions we have, that there are lots of people who are less fortunate than we are, and that for the most part we are making ends meet. This may take the form of a simple daily

Specific to my work situation (I am a public school speech therapist, married with two teenage children), it seems there is never enough of me, my time, or my effort. There are *always* more students to serve, more classroom teachers to consult with or placate, more parents to talk to (but first I must track them down), more things to read, more lessons to prepare, more student teachers to train, more articles to write.

How do I cope? Not really well all the time, I admit; but I do feel a sacred duty to give my best when I am engaged in any of the multiple parts of my job—whether it is differential diag-nosis of a disorder while I am face-to-face with a struggling student, writing an evaluation that will be used to deter-mine a student's treatment, counseling a parent or a student teacher, teaching a class of at-risk kindergartners, or engaging in one-on-one speech therapy with an unintelligible preschool child.

As I get older, I find that the strength to do all this comes only when I set limits. It requires that I say "no" to the less essential and focus on those tasks that "get more bang for the buck." Being prayerful helps me do this, but I am sel-dom sure that the others to whom I say "no" feel it is very spiritual of me!

Maureen McCarron—speech pathologist, wife, and mother Conesus, New York

prayer, a plaque or saying in our workplace that reminds us that we have enough, or even recognition of our paychecks as holy objects.

I have practiced one little discipline for many years. The first time each day that some-one asks me for money on the street, I give either fifty cents or a dollar. I have long since stopped worrying about whether or not this is good social policy. I figure that my meager amount will neither make nor break the person I give it to. Instead, I use these encounters as reminders that whatever possessions I have at the time are more than enough.

This "being satisfied with what we have," however, is not enough. We still have to deal with our desire for more things and more money. This desire is not inherently bad. It keeps our economy humming and can, in fact, lift everyone's boat if the proper social safe-guards are in place. But there are cases in which, as indi-viduals, we must decide what is enough and then stick to it in order to save our very souls. There are jobs, for example, that we quit or that we shouldn't take in the first place, even if the pay and benefits are good. Sometimes it is a matter of pursuing our talents, even if the marketplace does not value them. A classic example of this is the "starving artist" who quits a job in business or government to pursue his or her art, despite the financial sacrifices that entails. For people like that, whatever they make will have to be enough so that they can pursue their passion.

Other jobs are just not worth anyone's doing them, even if they pay very well. Manufacturing and marketing cigarettes, for example, might now be a career that no one should have. There are many other examples of jobs that, for ethical or moral reasons, people should not do.

For most of us, however, the question of deciding what is enough money and sticking to it is not a matter of morality or of philosophical principle. It is much simpler than that. We have to decide how much "stuff" we need—and what we are willing to do to get it. If we need to be rich—however we define that—then we have pretty much committed ourselves to a certain set of economic decisions. If it is enough for us to be middle-class, then we have to maintain that standard of income. Even then, however, we have to decide which things we will consider to be luxuries and which to be necessities. If we must have a fifty-thousand-dollar car or must send our children to an Ivy League school, then these priorities will determine how much we

This is a story of a wise boss I once had. A sensitive policy problem had arisen late one Friday afternoon (as they often do in the thorny world of a state welfare bureau). Several of us were discussing the problem with a commissioner in his office. I was wound up and ready to endure angst over the weekend, but at one point my boss looked at his watch and said, "It's five minutes to Monday morning. We'll resume this discussion then."

In marvelously few words, he taught me how to let go and to protect my family as he protected his. I have tried to live by his example ever since, even while allowing room for true emergencies that do blur the line between company time and personal time. We need balance, of course. Backbone, yet flexibility. Avoiding both rigidity and flabbiness. For that we need spirit and the Spirit.

Paul Provencher—social worker, husband, and father, Norwood, Massachusetts consider to be enough. If we decide to live a modest lifestyle or even to live close to poverty, then this will limit our need to make a lot of money, but we will have to be content to live without a lot of things and not be envious of others.

The key to all of these decisions is to practice the discipline of deciding what is enough and sticking to it. This may mean writing down our financial goals each year and having a family meeting to discuss and adopt them. It may mean reviewing our financial situation each time we are offered a new job, a promotion, or even a raise. It may mean reviewing on a regular basis how much we really need for ourselves and how much we are sharing with others.

Enough Time

We also have to decide how much time is "enough." Of that too we have only a finite amount, and we must figure out how much of it we are going to spend on any one pursuit.

For most of us, our paid employment is the largest consumer of our time. Often our decision about how much money is enough has a direct impact on how much of our time we spend working. Overtime, second jobs, two-career marriages—these are tied to how much money we need. But sometimes we work, or at least keep working, not for the money but for the excitement, the prestige, the power, even for the good we are doing for others. At some point, however, we've got to step back and ask ourselves how much of the time we are spending at work is enough, and then we must act on that decision. Two other disciplines of the spirituality of work can help us do that: living with our imperfection and balancing our work, personal, family, church, and community responsibilities.

It is not only in our paid employment that we have to decide how much time is enough. In everything we do, from sleeping, to raising children, to pursuing hobbies and leisure activities, to maintaining our homes, we have to decide how much time is enough. For example, I love to coach my children's sports teams, and at one point I found myself coaching so much that it was interfering with my work, my relationship with my wife, my other volunteer activities, and even the time I try to reserve for myself. So I made a decision to limit myself to coaching only baseball (my favorite), and I have stuck to that decision. Not surprisingly, this has been good for my spiritual life, but my kids have also benefited, both from experiencing other coaches and from having me more relaxed and focused whether I am coaching them or cheering for them from the sidelines.

One of the biggest wastes of time is watching television, and surfing the Internet is probably not far behind. I know hardly anyone, myself included, who does not feel that he or she spends too much time in front of a screen. We know that the entertainment value just isn't that high. Yet we continue to lose valuable time to television and the Web. Why? Because we aren't disciplined. We have not decided what is enough and

The nature of my work is such that it's never done at the end of the day. At best, by the end of the day I finish a major task or reach a good breaking point. My worst end-of-the-day problem is deciding how to respond to informal meetings that wander all over the map and often have an element of socializing as well. What is "enough" is a big problem here.

Another end-of-the-day problem is the fact that I am single and live alone, with no daily responsibilities to other people at home. I have occasional community and church activities in the evening, but I don't have a significant reason to leave the office at a reasonable time on a daily basis.

A few jobs ago, I discovered how short-lived most "work products" really are. I had been at this job for six years and had built some wonderful computer systems, establishing good methods and procedures and providing a lot of training—both formal and casual—to my fellow employees. Suddenly things changed, mostly due to a new manager. In less than a year, all of my "work products" had been destroyed. It was a very disheartening experience, but remembering it has helped me keep perspective on how much investment I make in my work.

Celeste Francis—management information systems consultant, Los Angeles, California then stuck to it. I do know some people who limit themselves to one hour a day on the computer or to one or two shows per week on television, but for most of us who complain that we don't have enough time to do the things we say we want to do, television watching and Internet surfing account for much lost time.

We will never have enough time until we decide what is enough time to be spending on the various activities of our lives. The disciplines of the spirituality of work can help us do that, and they can help us carry out our decisions.

Enough Effort and Success (or Failure)

As with money and time, we have to decide how much effort on a particular project is enough, and part of that decision is based on the amount of success we aspire to or the amount of failure we will tolerate. If a business sets a goal of a 10-percent increase in sales for a year, this can be either realistic or unrealistic, based on the marketing strategy, the quality of the products, the efficiency of the employees, and so forth. But there are also factors over which the company has absolutely no control, such as the overall economy, the work of the competition, natural disasters, or the illness, death, or defection of a key employee.

Depending on how much effort the company puts in, the 10-percent increase can most likely be achieved. The question that has to be asked is "How much success (or, alternatively, how much failure) is enough?" If it means that everyone puts in massive amounts of overtime or that supervisors put undue pressure on employees, this might well create an atmosphere of fear and competition among the staff. It might even risk the ongoing viability of the firm itself. In this situation, the effort to achieve the increase may not be worth it. Someone has to step in and say, "Enough! Maybe the goal was too high, maybe the internal or external situation has changed dramatically, maybe it was just a mistake, but in any case we have put in enough effort on this project. A five-percent increase will have to be enough success."

The same scenario can play out in our private lives or individual jobs. Sometimes we beat our heads against a wall to accomplish something when the only truly spiritual decision is to say that we have put in enough effort and that we will just have to live with the success we have achieved. We have to mow half the lawn or shovel half the driveway, receive a B instead of an A, lose the account, settle for a modest increase or accept a modest decrease, come in third place, leave the dirty dishes in the sink until morning.

There is a spiritual side to this seeming failure. We can fall back on the notion that it is not by our effort alone that we succeed, that God has a part in all our work, and that failure and incompleteness are part of the human condition. There are many practices that can help us reach this state of enlightenment. For example, before we start a task we can set a time limit and hold to it, no matter what the result. We can share the work with others and also the decision about

Enough **has both** negative and positive connotations. The negative meaning comes out in a phrase such as "not the best, but good enough." Here the word implies setting a limitation that prevents us from attaining our highest goal. It suggests settling for an easier, less demanding way that doesn't bring out our full capabilities.

The other meaning of enough is very different. Here the word points to the golden mean between two extremes. "Enough" in this context signifies the ideal balance between "too much" and "too little." Having spent half my life in a Chinese-speaking world with its yin-yang spirituality, this way of understanding "enough" is very important to me. In this perspective, "enough" signifies "harmony"—the harmony that stands between the stridency of too much and the slackness of too little.

The image that comes to my mind is that of tuning in my FM receiver to listen to music. There's a perfect frequency on the band where everything is in tune and beautiful, harmonious sound pours out. On each side of that frequency is buzz and distortion. Putting our lives in harmony with God's mission for us is that node that defines the "enough" between extremes. Here is where we find the resonance that empowers without stressing. The most beautiful singing is done when the throat and body are most relaxed. Understood in this sense, "enough" isn't a halfway compromise. It's the goal.

Peyton G. Craighill—Episcopal priest, husband, and father, Narberth, Pennsylvania when to say "enough." We can keep track of our failures and successes and review them once a year, recognizing how modest most of them really were.

Maybe once a day we need to have a bell go off (literally or in our heads), at which time we look at whatever we are doing at the time and ask ourselves, "Have I done enough on this? Have I tried hard enough? Have I had enough success (or failure) at this?" If the answer is no, then the follow-up question should be "When will enough be enough?"

Enough Spirituality

Here is a really hard question for those of us who take religion and spirituality seriously. When have we had enough of it? In many ways, this is a silly question. Spirituality is not like money, time, effort, or even success. How can we ever have enough spirituality? What would enough spirituality look like? How can we say that we have done enough to align ourselves and our environment with God?

In one sense, we can't. Paul told us to "pray unceasingly." But the whole idea of the spirituality of work is that it can be practiced right in the midst of our daily activities and that it is more a matter of awareness than of pious practices. All of this is true, yet sometimes we can still feel that we have somehow not done enough in the spiritual life, even if we were trying our best and practicing all kinds of disciplines to help us.

I was once asked to give a retreat for a group of businesspeople in Hartford, Connecticut. Since I was the first layperson to be asked, I was honored to accept. I then received a call from the priest organizing the retreat, who said that the planning committee had met and wanted me to give a "Jesus-centered retreat on the spirituality of work." My initial reaction was that I didn't think I could do so. I am no Bible scholar, and I had never thought much about Jesus as a role model for the spirituality of work. While it is true that tradition has him working as a carpenter for the first thirty years of his life, we really don't know much about those hidden years. During his lifetime he was an itinerant preacher with no visible means of support, with no wife and children, and—as he said himself—with not even a place to lay his head. What did Jesus have to say to those of us struggling to make sense of our work and balance it with the rest of our lives?

I was ready to tell the committee that I could not give the retreat when I happened to read a quote from Albert Einstein, who said that the mark of a true genius is the ability to hold two contradictory thoughts in one's mind at the same time. For some reason, this connected with my problem of Jesus and the spirituality of work. I thought, *If Jesus was a genius (and I assume he was), what were the two contradictory thoughts he held in his mind at the same time?* I came up with several pairs of ideas, but the one that jumped out at me in terms of work was this: What if Jesus believed that—at any given time and at exactly the same time—we have never done enough and yet have already done enough?

As I began to look at some of the Gospel stories with this contradiction in mind, they began to make sense to me for the first time. I thought of the laborers in the field, the rich young man, the woman at the well, and so on. In so many stories, Jesus seemed to be saying that if we think we have done enough, we have not, and if we think we have not done enough, we already have.

This contradiction seemed to fit the struggles I was having with the ambiguities of the spirituality of work, and so I agreed to use it as the theme for the retreat. The idea seemed to ring true to the experience of the participants, and it has since become the basis for my own understanding and practice.

It seems to me that whatever our work, we need to build into it ways of reminding ourselves that there are self-imposed limits to what we need or want or are capable of. We have to determine what those limits are and stick to them if we are to be in touch with God, who is always "enough."

Practicing the Discipline

- Write down on a piece of paper how much money you need to live on. Put it with your income-tax file and review and update it each year. Note the discrepancy (if any) between what you earned and what you think is enough.

- Each time you are offered a promotion, a raise, or a new job, ask for time to consider the offer and then pray over whether or not you want it and the price you might have to pay for taking it.

- Make a list of jobs you don't think anyone should have. If yours is on it, start looking for another job.

- Make a list of your "greatest failures," that is, goals you did not accomplish that later turned out to be not so important. (In fact, it may have been for the better that you didn't accomplish them.) Keep the list posted in your workplace and add to it regularly.

- Whenever you decide that you have not spent enough time or effort on a project, ask yourself what will be "enough." Write that down and stick to it.

- Listen to the Sunday Scripture readings, especially the Gospel passage, in light of the contradiction "You have never done enough; you have already done enough."

Chapter 10

Balancing Work, Personal, Family, Church, and Community Responsibilities

Earth's crammed with heaven
And every common bush afire with God;
But only he who sees, takes off his shoes.

Elizabeth Barrett Browning

No one works in only one arena. Most of us have jobs, family responsibilities, personal interests, and church and community involvements. And often our different responsibilities are in competition. We need to develop some way of reviewing each situation and deciding what we really need to do. Is one of our children having trouble in school? Are we under special stress at work because of a big threat or an opportunity? Do we need more time with a friend or spouse or by ourselves? Is there a crisis in our community or church that must be addressed?

Once we have taken this inventory, we then have to recognize that every one of these responsibilities is worthy of our time and effort. For the most part, we are not called upon to choose between good things and bad things. Rather, we are forced to juggle many good things, and we try to attend to them as conscientiously as we can while we acknowledge and accept our own limitations.

Many religious commentators would claim that balancing responsibilities is simply a matter of putting family first. For some, this may in fact be what is needed, but it is not necessarily the problem—or the solution—for most of us in achieving spiritual balance in our daily lives. We are all familiar with the addiction we call workaholism, where someone puts his or her work before everything else. Few people defend this practice, although there are many firms and companies in which it is rewarded and even expected. But we all know people who focus on family to the extent that they allow their personal lives, their community involvement, their participation in church, and even their paid employment to suffer. None of these imbalances are spiritually healthy, and our task is to practice a discipline that helps us keep all our responsibilities in balance.

Saying No

One practice that might help us balance our responsibilities is the simple act of saying no. Many of us get ourselves in trouble just because of our inability to say this little word often enough. On our jobs, it may be a matter of refusing a specific assignment, promotion, transfer, or new job if we know that we can't do it without causing real harm to the people in our lives, including ourselves.

At home, we might have to say no to our children joining another traveling sports team or to putting that addition on the house or to making a high-risk investment that would put additional pressure on our family finances should it fail. At a certain point or in a certain manner, we might say no to retiring (or to continuing to work, for that matter). We might even need to say no to our children when they want to attend an expensive college or have a big wedding or (God forbid) have us raise that child they had out of wedlock. Agreeing to any or all of the above might make it impossible for us to fulfill our other obligations in life.

The same kind of discipline might have to happen with our church and community involvement. It may be very gratifying to have our names put forth to head this committee or run for that office, but if our lives are out of balance it can only lead to problems at work, with our families, or within ourselves. It never ceases to amaze me how insensitive many church professionals are to this problem. While they are encouraging people to spend more time with their families and to spread the Good News in the workplace, many think nothing of allowing or even encouraging people to volunteer five, ten, even twenty hours a week. In fact, in much the same way that businesses reward workaholics, religious institutions tend to praise and reward "churchaholics" for their overinvolvement at church.

I once belonged to a parish that had an annual Ministry Sunday. A long list of more than fifty ministries the parish sponsors was handed out in the pews, and the priest gave an impassioned homily on the importance of contributing our "time" and "talent" as well as our "treasure" to the church. Right in the middle of the service we all stopped to sign up for one or more of the ministries.

I had no real problem with this, and my wife and I volunteered for a couple of ministries in which we were already involved. A couple of weeks later, however, I saw the following headline in our parish newsletter: "Pew Potatoes Lose 61 to Parish Ministries." As I

Ever since my children (now three and a half and six years old, respectively) were born, I have made a lot of changes in my life to try to balance these very demanding new responsibilities. I do most of the cooking when I get home after work, then I help the boys get ready for bed. When I am home I always give them their baths and read them their bedtime stories. When I am not working on the weekends, Saturday is "daddy day" for my two boys. I let their mom sleep in and I take the boys grocery shopping. After we get home and put the groceries away, we all go on cheap field trips (which are chosen by the two of them).

In terms of travel, I have simply said no to trips that were not essential to my work. Instead, I have sent others to a number of national meetings that did not strictly require my presence. I have negotiated with coworkers in my office to have them take longer-distance travel assignments so that I can be at home more often. For trips that I absolutely have to make, I try my best to minimize the nights away from home. For a conference that begins at 9:00 a.m., for example, I used to fly the prior afternoon in order to have a relaxing start to the event. Now I have become (against my proclivities) an early-morning person and take predawn flights to avoid being away from home that extra night.

In terms of my personal well-being, I work out at a gym two or three days a week. It is a great stress reliever as well as a way of keeping my body in halfway decent shape. On the weekends, I only go to the gym when the boys are having their nap or quiet time. Prayer often gets lost in the shuffle. Perhaps the best way that I pray is during men's choir at my parish—one-hour practices on Wednesday evenings and during liturgy on Sundays. This is the one personal involvement that I guard jealously. I often find myself too tired—if not physically, then mentally—to do much of anything else. For example, I have not balanced my checkbook in over a year, and our house (especially my parts of it) is often a huge mess. But I feel that it is very important to be a strong presence in my children's lives as well as an equal partner in my marriage. The affection of my family is a great payoff to my demanding schedule.

Michael Stone—diocesan staffperson, husband, and father
Richmond, Virginia

read further, it turned out that "the Pew Potatoes lost sixty-one parishioners who got out of their pews, stood up, and were counted in with the more than five hundred parishioners who already give of their time and talent in the many ministries that make [our parish] the outstanding parish that it is."

What struck me was the assumption that anyone who was not volunteering for the parish was lazy and wrong—likened to a "couch potato" who does nothing but sit around and watch television. But what if among some of those nonvolunteers there was a business owner who was working overtime to save a company and its fifty jobs, or a man or woman who was sandwiched between two generations and caring for both, or someone who was running an important political campaign, or somebody who was just plain "burned out"? Do we really want such people to add to their stress by volunteering for a church ministry? And when they don't volunteer, do they really deserve to be labeled "pew potatoes"?

Saying no is sometimes difficult. We hate to disappoint others. We agree that the job needs to be done by someone, and we want to do our fair share. We even think that perhaps if we just organize our time a little better, we might be able to say yes. But if we don't practice saying no, we usually aren't helping anyone, and we most certainly are contributing to the imbalance in our lives. Unless we are wasting a lot of our time already, something usually has to give if we take on another responsibility, and we are better off admitting it than fooling ourselves and disappointing others.

Two little disciplines I try to practice are to say one no for every yes and to drop one job or responsibility for each new one I take on. Those who know me will attest that saying no is very difficult for me, but if I do not do it then I find my life getting severely out of balance. (What I often try to "cheat" on is time for myself or time for myself and my wife to be alone together. This almost always leads to disastrous results!)

So try it. Put your tongue to the roof of your mouth, make an "nnnn" sound, and then make your lips round and say "ooooh." Now put the sounds together and say "no" with feeling.

Keeping Our Promises

Of course, we cannot say no to everything, nor should we. Our daily work in many ways must be a series of yeses if we are to be in communion with the God of generosity, the God who said yes and continues saying yes to creation. When someone in our workplace asks us to do something, we need to be able to respond positively whenever possible. For example, when a colleague or boss requests our help at work on a special project or during an emergency, we need to be able to comply without risking throwing our entire lives out of balance. The same is true for demands made by our families, our churches, our community groups, and our personal needs.

Not only do we need to be able to say yes in these situations but we also need to be able to follow through on our promises. This requires the spiritual discipline of "institutionalizing" our good intentions. Please stick with me on this, because it is a spiritual practice that I have found extremely important in helping me balance my various responsibilities.

It seems to me that the big problem in balancing our lives is not that we don't want to do the right thing. It is not even that others— our families, our colleagues or employers, those in charge of the various church and secular organizations to which we belong—want us to feel pressured, out of balance, tense, worried, or unhappy. These are pretty unproductive states, and they very often lead to complete burnout so that we are of no use to anyone. Others don't really want us to be this way. They just want us to do what we said we'd do.

So once we've learned to say no when we need to, we've then got to make our yeses work. In order to make that happen, we've got to institutionalize our decisions. What do I mean by institutionalize? I mean create a way, a practice, a discipline, or a schedule by which we insure that we do what we say we are going to do.

Here is an example. More than twelve years ago, my wife, Kathy, and I had twins, followed twenty months later by a third child. We realized very quickly that our spousal relationship, which we both value greatly, could very easily get lost in all the work of childrearing.

For a period, my life became top-heavy with work. That didn't mean that my family and friends couldn't be kept up-to-date on what I was doing and what my feelings were about it. I always had lots of stories about my work. Most of them were hard for my family and friends to believe, but they could participate in my work through listening to the stories.

I think that telling and listening to stories is part of the key to spiritual balance. Stories are what we can share between one sphere of our lives and the others. My work stories touch or inform my family life or civic activity or church involvement stories, and vice versa. If I don't see and tell these stories, then the various parts of my life do not connect with the other parts and I end up a fragmented man.

My stories are always social—even when I think they are only about me. They are the story of community. It's crucial for me to realize the roles my faith community, my family community, my spousal community, my workplace community, my civic community, the national community, and the world community play in my life and to realize that, ultimately, they are all one community. The Pima Indians say, "God made the universe. Come and see it." These various communities that connect in my life ultimately touch the source of them all: God.

The reign of God is big stuff. It contains God's bigheartedness. If I'm rooted in God's reign then I'm rooted in nature, in city life, in family, in church, in work, in civic outreach. I can't leave *any* of the parts of my life out if I am to take part in God's bigheartedness. I can't focus on all of them all the time, but my awareness of each, and sharing the stories of my participation in each, sustains me in the others.

James C. Rooney—retired publisher, husband, father, and grandfather
Evanston, Illinois

I have needed to sacrifice a lot of my personal time in order to do the work I consider essential for the continued promotion of peace and justice in a city and church that are experiencing unparalleled growth of diverse populations. My family understands that this is a crucial point in time to do "prevention" work in promoting peaceful multicultural relations, and they are proud to back me up by doing without me on many occasions.

On the positive side of my struggle for balance in my life, I have made great strides in my process of "growing up" by finding out what my vocation is and living up to that vocation. I have learned to dismiss a lot of the guilt feelings that crop up when I choose either my work or my family over the other. I continue to remind myself that sometimes it is my own marginalization that I have to struggle against. Not only do I take time to defend the rights of other workers to spend time with their families, but I also remember that when I defend my own and my family's rights to the same thing I am defending the rights of other justice workers who follow me. When I insist on a fair wage for myself, I stand up for those workers whose families live just above or below the poverty level because they cannot get a decent wage from the church. In defending others' dignity I've learned to defend my own, and vice versa.

Nylda Dieppa-Aldarondo—homemaker, pastoral minister, wife, and mother
Maitland, Florida

We vowed that this would never happen, but we had to institutionalize that decision for it to be effective. We knew that we needed regular time together without the kids that was focused just on us and our relationship. So we established an every-other-Saturday-night date, which we put on our calendar. We then lined up babysitters for those Saturday nights way in advance. (We had one girl who started with us when she was a freshman in high school and worked for us on and off through college. I figured out at one point that we had spent more than five thousand dollars on babysitting over a ten-year period.)

This discipline had several results. First, Kathy and I came to treasure those Saturday-night dates. Sometimes we planned something, but often we just went out to dinner or to a bookstore. Near Christmas, we would do our Christmas shopping together. Second, our children were comfortable right from the start with having a babysitter, and they also came to understand that it is a normal thing for parents to have time alone together. In fact, they still refer to our "dates" without the least bit of embarrassment or self-consciousness. Finally, Kathy's and my commitment to our relationship has endured and strengthened, due in no small part to this little spiritual practice. We have done what we said we wanted to do on this little thing, and that same spirit has transferred to the bigger things in our marriage.

This same kind of discipline can be practiced in all the spheres of our lives. When we make any commitment, we need to institutionalize our intentions. At work, for example, if we say that we want to do long-range strategic planning, then we have to schedule it into our annual calendars, hire a facilitator, and figure out some way to cover our ongoing business while we do it. In fact, our datebooks can be a wonderful way of institutionalizing our intentions and keeping our promises to others and to ourselves. When we make a decision to do something, the very next step ought to be to pull out our calendars and schedule the meetings necessary to make it happen.

I used to consult with community organizers, all of whom said that they wanted to reflect regularly on their own development. I recommended that they institutionalize that decision by committing themselves to reflect about their work for one-and-a-half hours per week and write their reflections into a report that they shared with me when we met. Every one of them made that commitment,

> **I have a very irregular** schedule at work, so it is hard to keep track of how many hours I actually work in a week. Many, many years ago, I developed the discipline of keeping an account of my work hours on my calendar. Hours with a circle are my main, full-time work, and hours with boxes are all the outside freelance jobs I take in addition to my job. Each Saturday I add up the circles and boxes and once a month I total them. Whenever I surpass an average of sixty hours per week for a month, I begin to take additional time off with my family. This has been the sole tool I use to help me manage the enormous amount of work I have.
>
> **Michael Galligan-Stierle**—director of campus ministry, husband, and father
> Wheeling, West Virginia

but most of them failed to do it. They had all kinds of reasons why they did not do what they said they wanted to do, but basically it came down to a failure to institutionalize their decision. I would suggest that if they really were serious about reflecting, then they had to schedule those ninety-minute sessions in their datebooks for fifty-two weeks in advance. That way, when they arrived at the "appointment with themselves" on their calendars, they remembered their commitment, and while they were free to move their reflection to another time during that week, they at least could not say that they forgot to do it. I found that those who institutionalized their decision to reflect did so, and those who did not, did not.

By institutionalizing our decisions, we are able to keep our promises—to ourselves and to others—about what we value and what we will do with our time, effort, and attention. This is one of the spiritual disciplines that will allow us to balance our various responsibilities.

Learning Flexibility

Another discipline that will help us keep our promises is flexibility. Being flexible is not the same as rationalizing our failure to keep our promises. It is a matter of being able to give a little in one area of our life so that we can fulfill our responsibilities in another.

One discipline I have is to try to be home for dinner almost every night by six o'clock. This very often means that I must leave much work undone (see the chapter on living with imperfection), but it does force me to live by values about personal and family life that I claim to espouse. But there are times when I have to be flexible with this rule, or it will rule me. Sometimes it is necessary to work late or go to a meeting directly from work. My wife and children understand this, partly because I work at keeping my promise to be home most nights and partly because I am equally flexible when it comes to their needs.

The spiritual discipline of flexibility, then, might require that we force ourselves to reflect each time one of the parts of our life asks the others to be "understanding." It may then be time for some trade-offs and compromises, including deciding what is enough in any one area and sticking to it.

Much has been written in recent years about the importance of having "quality time" in all areas of our lives, and it is certainly true that it does little good to be physically present to others but psychologically and spiritually absent. Quality time does not just happen. It requires planning, coordination of schedules, assembling needed materials, and so forth. It also requires that we be well rested, as stress free as possible, and focused on the task at hand.

The discipline of balancing our responsibilities, however, is not only about quality time and effort. It is also about *quantity* time and effort. Part of being spiritually present— on our jobs, with our families, in our communities or churches—is just being there and available. There are certain times when we need to

---

When my dad was in the workforce, most men (and I say that because most career people were male) got a job with a company and stayed there until retirement. Now it is estimated that most people will work for as many as four different employers in their lifetime. Many people not only move from one company to another but from one location to someplace far away.

But the big difference is that the term "breadwinner" is quickly fading from use. Balancing work and family often involves not just a husband's career but the wife's as well. This adds a new dynamic to the discussion. If I am asked to take on a managerial role, for example, especially if it includes relocation, the decision cannot be made on the basis of my career alone. My wife's must also be taken into consideration. Even if relocation is not required, we have to discuss whether the new position might add stress to the family. We have to decide what comes first, the need to advance and make more money or the need to keep our family happy in nonmaterial ways. People used to celebrate promotions with great exuberance, and some still do. But now even the best moves need to be considered in light of family needs, and balance has become an important word.

Michael J. Hogan—sales consultant and husband, Evergreen Park, Illinois

> **Balance is best** achieved when all parts of our lives are spiritual. Being courteous is spiritual. Playing by the rules is spiritual. Being on time, doing your job, playing your role are all spiritual. Not making one part of your life pay for another is spiritual.
>
> **Nancy M. Botteri**—certified public accountant, wife, and mother Portland, Oregon

hang around, not doing much perhaps but being part of the group. It may be shooting the breeze with a coworker, shooting hoops with a child, stopping for coffee after Sunday services, or marching in the local Fourth of July parade, but it is often in the midst of such "quantity" time that "quality" time happens.

A discipline that might help us achieve balance in our lives is to make sure that we do things that we might otherwise consider a waste of time. I practice this with my three children by stopping at least once a day before saying no to something they want me to do and asking myself "Why not?" Often I end up saying yes. In the workplace, flexibility can be as simple as rescheduling a meeting, postponing a deadline, giving someone a second chance, or redefining success. But remember, the point of flexibility is to help ourselves and others achieve spiritual balance in our lives, not to increase the imbalance.

Balancing Responsibilities

Here is a story told to me by statistician David Fluharty that pretty much sums up this discipline of the spirituality of work.

> It is certainly easy to get caught up in work and professional activities on one hand. On the other hand, we can let other activities and the demands of family lead to slighting responsibilities to our work. Each action must be considered individually and in the context of balancing all that one is doing. It is difficult to make decisions in light of "the greater scheme of things," however, and sometimes we do not know how important a single act of making the right decision will seem to us later on.

This is the story of one such action I took. Although it seemed small at the time, it is one of the decisions of which I am most proud in my life. Some years ago, a meeting for my industry was scheduled in another city on a topic about which I have a great deal of interest and some expertise. Thus, I really wanted to participate fully. However, on the evening of the meeting, there was to be an annual picnic and overnight campout at my daughter's elementary school. I wanted to be back in time for this, as it seemed very important to my daughter. I had a good relationship with the person for whom I worked at the time, and he supported my decision to leave the meeting at noon to fly back and pick up my daughter for the event. We were a little late for the picnic and I missed half of my meeting, but it was an attempt to balance two important responsibilities.

There were three important lessons I learned from this episode. The first is the importance of the workplace environment in our ability to balance work and family. Because of the support of my management, my decision to be with my daughter was not difficult to make. I can imagine many managers who would not be so understanding and many companies in which an "understanding" manager would be criticized. Some employees are probably inhibited from even suggesting the possibility of leaving such a meeting early for such an "insignificant" reason. While I hope that I would have made the same decision in a less supportive environment, there is no way to know for sure.

I am eternally grateful to the man for whom I worked for his support of my decision, and this gratitude may seem a little out of proportion until you consider the second lesson I learned. Within two years of this picnic and campout, my daughter died suddenly. Because of the decision I had made and the support I had received from my boss, I now have a wonderful and comforting memory of juggling my schedule to participate in a fun event with my daughter, rather than having to endure the pain of looking back with regret at what I should have done.

The third lesson I learned is that people in management may not realize the tremendous impact they can have for good, even on relatively simple matters, if they, too, value their employees keeping balance in their lives. After all, it is difficult to imagine that my leaving the meeting early made much difference to the other participants—I had given at least my fair share of input before noon anyway. But being with my daughter that day made all the difference in the world to me and to her.

Saying no, saying yes. Keeping our promises, being flexible. Quality time, quantity time. These sound like contradictions, but they are more like the opposite ends of the long pole that a tightrope walker uses to stay balanced. All of the decisions we have to make in our work each day can be exhausting if we are trying to decide the "right" thing to do in every situation. The practices of the discipline of balancing, however, can take some of those decisions away, or at least give us a basis for making them.

Practicing the Discipline

- Say no ten times in the mirror each morning. Then look for one opportunity each day to say no for real.

- Before you say yes to a new responsibility, decide which present responsibility you are willing and able to give up.

- Make a list of the one major promise in each of the spheres of your life that you want to keep. Once a week, pull out your calendar and decide what you need to schedule in order to keep those promises.

- For one month, keep track of which areas of your life are being asked to "give" for the sake of other areas. If one area predominates, then make sure, for the following month, that all your other responsibilities are the ones that make the adjustments.

- Plan some quality time in one area of responsibility that you have been neglecting. Then spend some quantity time in the same area. Compare the results.

Chapter 11

Working to Make "The System" Work

We simply spend too much time and have too much psychic and emotional energy invested in the workplace for us to declare that it is a spiritual desert bereft of life-giving water.

David Whyte

This next discipline is the toughest, the most controversial, the most frustrating, often the least successful, yet perhaps the most necessary of all within the spirituality of work. "Making the system work" in Christian parlance is called "social justice." Jewish tradition uses the phrase *tikkun olam,* which can be translated as "mending the fabric of the world." Buddhism has a phrase, "right living," that also captures this idea. No major world religion that I have studied has failed to have this concept as a prominent part of its teaching.

No spirituality is legitimate that does not incorporate social justice in some form, for otherwise spirituality becomes individualistic navel-gazing or piety that does not address the context in which the spiritual is practiced. This is even more true, I believe, if we are trying to practice a spirituality based on our daily work.

One Scenario

Let's take the case of a female nurse in a large hospital. That nurse may practice every one of the disciplines I have mentioned. She may surround herself with sacred objects to remind her of the deeper meaning of her work. She may have come to grips with her imperfection yet strives daily to ensure that she is doing the best work of which she is capable. She may regularly give thanks and congratulations, both to herself and to her colleagues, and she may work to build support and community within her workplace. She may deal with everyone—patients, families, doctors, other nurses, support staff—with kindness and compassion, just as she would like to be treated. She may have her priorities straight, adjusting her hours to her family's needs, taking time for herself, and volunteering at her church and for several community causes. She may keep up with the medical literature in her field and regularly take courses and seminars in personal and professional development.

Let's face it. The woman is a saint!

But . . . the hospital this nurse works in is completely disorganized. It is understaffed, underfunded, and short of space and supplies.

It has a deserved reputation for arrogance and indifference to the surrounding community. The medical staff is disillusioned and discouraged and has begun sniping at the administration. The administration has a high turnover rate, and the hospital has recently been bought out by a huge hospital system that has promised to cut costs drastically. The employee unions, including the nurses association, seem interested only in collecting dues and protecting workers from disciplinary actions. And the hospital buildings themselves are old and in great need of renovation.

Meanwhile, hundreds of thousands of people in the city have no health insurance. As a result, many are putting off primary and preventative care until their health has deteriorated to such an extent that they must enter a hospital, usually through the emergency room. The local, state, and federal governments have all cut back on health-care funding, and even Medicare and Medicaid are threatened with deep cuts. Many of the insurance and managed-care programs associated with the hospital seem much more interested in denying claims than in providing additional care. And social problems

---

One of the ways many workers try to make the system work is by organizing a union. Workers join unions to be treated with dignity, to ensure safer working conditions, to have a voice in how work is organized, and to seek just wages and benefits. Unfortunately, it is hard for many workers to form unions. In the United States alone, more than ten thousand workers per year are fired for organizing.

My experience is that the leaders in most union-organizing drives are deeply spiritual people who are taking risks in order to improve the workplace for all. Nursing-home workers who organize a union, for example, almost always fight to have their patients treated better. Poultry workers want to ensure that food is handled safely for both the workers and the consumers.

Workers form unions for a voice in the workplace. Yes, people want better wages and benefits, but more importantly, they want to be treated respectfully.

Kim Bobo—director of interfaith committee for worker justice, wife, and mother
Chicago, Illinois

in the community surrounding the hospital—including poverty, violence, drugs, and disease—have increased the demand for and the seriousness of the health care this hospital should be providing.

Here is the point: This nurse, this saint whom everyone loves and who does her work in a competent manner every day, cannot do her best work, cannot realize her full spiritual potential, cannot "align herself and her environment with God" unless she practices the discipline of working to make the system work.

Let's see how she—and we—might do that.

Social Justice

"The system sucks!" "This organization is totally dysfunctional!" "Dilbert is right!" How many times have you heard (or said) something like this in your workplace? How about "All politicians are corrupt," or "You can't fight city hall," or "Don't vote, it only encourages them"? Even in church circles you hear similar cries of frustration and passivity: "This church is going to hell in a handbasket."

This is where the virtue of social justice comes in. It is the grace to stand up and fight to maintain what is right and to change what is wrong in the institutions of work, family, church, and society for the good of their members and the community at large. Social justice seeks to transform the world, to help bring about the kingdom of God on earth, if you will. It is only through the practice of social justice that the institutions of society and church are continuously being structured and restructured to be more responsive to human needs. As Ron Krietmeyer, director of the Office for Social Justice of the Archdiocese of St. Paul, Minnesota, has said, "Social justice is not individual. It is social and relational. That is to say, social justice is not about private, individual acts. It is about collective actions aimed at transforming social institutions and structures in order to achieve the common good."

Unfortunately, social justice (or "social action," as it is sometimes called) has gotten a bad name among a lot of people because we have come to equate it with "outsider" protest movements, that is, protest by people outside of the institutions of power. This is certainly one form of social justice. The abolition movement, the peace movement, the women's liberation movement, the civil rights movement, and the antiabortion movement are all examples of people fighting for social justice from "outside" the system. Tactics of these movements almost always include protests, confrontation, sometimes even civil disobedience of one kind or another.

It is important for all of us to recognize that this form of social justice is sometimes the only one available to people, especially those who have been disenfranchised by the very system that is supposed to serve them. While we may disagree with a particular tactic or not feel comfortable ourselves with participating in these movements, we should recognize that it is sometimes the only route people have. In fact, participating in such social justice efforts may well be an important element in our spiritual lives.

The mistake, I believe—and one that has been pointed out consistently by the National Center for the Laity in Chicago—is to limit social action to these "outsider" movements. It is equally important to work for social justice from "inside" the institutions of church and society. The nurse in our example can probably do much more good for social justice if she remains a nurse, continues to work at the hospital where she currently works, and struggles from within the system to make it a better place. The same goes for people in almost every profession and occupation. Politics may be corrupt, but that's all the more reason we need good politicians, just as we need good movie producers, good cabdrivers, good engineers—good everything.

Such "insider" social justice is accessible to all of us. And while it may be less dramatic and even less heroic than the "outsider" version, it can be equally effective. As the U.S. Catholic bishops have said, "The most common, and in many ways, the most important Christian witness is often neither very visible nor highly structured. It is the sacrifice of parents trying to raise children with concern for others, the service and creativity of workers who do their best and reach out to

Every institution devised by human beings is in need of Christ's transforming love and grace. Many of us have been duped into thinking that the institutions designed to get and consolidate power (business, politics) are somehow inherently less worthy of our time, energy, and talents than those explicitly created to "do good," such as the church or charitable, educational, or health-care institutions. This dichotomy is a false one and, I believe, it has the ironic effect of anesthetizing the vast majority of us engaged or employed in "power" institutions from unleashing the transforming and redemptive power of Christ in those realms.

Until we become really convinced that gospel values and the gospel message belong everywhere, we will not evangelize our offices, law firms, factories, or banks. We evangelize most persuasively by the way we live our lives: how we spend our time and talents, who and what we love, how we vote and spend our money.

Kathleen McGarvey Hidy—lawyer, wife, and mother, Cincinnati, Ohio

those in need, the struggle of business owners trying to reconcile the bottom line and the needs of employees and customers, and the hard choices of public officials who seek to protect the weak and pursue the common good. The church's social mission is advanced by teachers and scientists, by family farmers and bankers, by salespersons and entertainers."

What should all these people be doing in their workplaces? First of all, they should be doing good work. This would mean practicing the various disciplines of work that we have been considering in this book, but that in itself would not be enough. Social justice in the workplace does not just happen. It is not just a matter of being a good person and doing a good job. It is a conscious effort to do what is necessary to ensure that the system itself is working—not just for us but for everyone. For the nurse in our example, it means not just being personally faithful and connected to God in her own work but also being effective in ensuring that the hospital itself is doing the same.

It is this need to be "effective" that scares a lot of people from acting on social justice. Good intentions, unfortunately, are not enough if we are to make the workplace more like the way God would have things. We need to work to make sure that it happens. Fortunately, the spirituality of work offers some practices that can help us in this discipline of working to make the system work.

Organization

"Organization is the act of social justice," says Bill Droel, the driving force behind the National Center for the Laity. By that he means that we cannot practice social justice in isolation. While there are examples of individuals standing up for what is right without support and without fear of the consequences (Jesus comes immediately to mind), martyrs are not the best role models for social justice. The apostle Paul was important in church history because he was an organizational genius, not because he was a martyr. While Peter and the other apostles sat around Jerusalem trying to figure out what to do next, Paul was out organizing local "chapters" in a string of important cities, and he was training local leaders to run them. It was Paul who recognized that if the Christian "system" was going to work, Gentiles were going to have to be welcomed into the church and that to do this effectively the Jewish custom of circumcision was going to have to be abandoned by the early Christians. So what did Paul do? He organized the first church council in Jerusalem, and there he lobbied for the reforms he thought were needed, even promising to

I currently work for a workers' compensation insurance company. I have observed attempts to make some of the processes into "assembly lines," and I have been asked to provide productivity statistics to enable this to happen. Each time I build a system along these lines, I provide some education on the appropriate use of data.

Whenever I perceive that my productivity statistics are being misused, I call people on it. If I'm not satisfied with the response, I escalate the issue. Sometimes this is an act of courage with significant risk. Other times it is merely a thoughtful response to a situation that I observe.

Celeste Francis—management information systems consultant, Los Angeles, California send to the church in Jerusalem all the alms he collected if the changes were adopted. Fortunately for us, Paul was effective, and the rest, as they say, is church history. (If you don't believe this story, read between the lines in Acts of the Apostles and Paul's letters.)

Organization is hard work. It means talking to lots of people, building relationships with them, understanding their self-interest, and joining them together in some structure that allows them to act in concert. It means going to lots of meetings, working out compromises, developing strategies, and planning and executing effective action. In some ways, organization can seem to take us away from our own work (and even our own spiritual lives). "I could do this easier myself!" we say, or "If I have to sit through one more meeting I think I'll scream."

Yet it is the very practice of organizing that allows us to discover the full spirituality of our work. For if we accept working in a system that is unjust, we cannot be fully connected with God, who is always just. It is our working to make the system work that actually makes the system work.

I practice this discipline by making sure that I am always involved in at least three organizations or committees at any one time: one in my industry, one in my church, and one in my community. I try to limit my involvement in these groups, because that is part of balancing my other responsibilities. In fact, part of the reason for organizing is that we can then count on others to do their share of the social justice work. Still, contributing to these efforts on an ongoing basis is part of my spiritual life—not a distraction from it.

Problems versus Issues

Another skill that helps us work for social justice is one I learned from community organizing. It is the ability to break problems down into issues that are identifiable and tangible enough to be dealt with.

One of the reasons people do not like to get involved in working to make the system work is that the task seems so overwhelming, even impossible. It is, if we are trying to solve all the problems of the world at once. Can we reform capitalism, save the environment, restructure the church, clean up politics, end poverty, bring about a peaceful world, and do everything else that is necessary to bring about the reign of God? Nope. Can we work on any or all of the problems we have and help make the world a little better place? Yep, but only if we learn to break down those problems into issues that we can do something about.

Let's go back to our hypothetical nurse one more time. Maybe she has realized how bad the health-care system is. Perhaps she has even committed herself to try to make it better. She may have organized her fellow nurses or made allies with the doctors, the patients, and the community. She may have even got the attention of the hospital owners and administrators as well as the business and government officials in her area. She is ready to do social

The most intractable problems in any system seem to be the individual foibles, resentments, intolerance, pride, and so forth that infect everything they touch and spread like plagues through the system.

So what if one person—somewhere, anywhere—in the system pauses and reflects on his or her own ego-ridden little power play or petty resentment? And what if that person actually chooses, as a result of that reflection, to behave in a more moderate, less ego-ridden, less resentful manner? Or perhaps—despite hesitancy, embarrassment, or a wish to avoid controversy—someone chooses not to remain silent in the workplace when some outrageous rumor or bigoted remark is uttered. Could this new style—spirituality if you will—also be infectious? Could it also have its ultimate effect in changing the system?

I realize that this may seem like small potatoes in the world of social justice, but I find this kind of effort to make the system better to be incredibly difficult. It compels me to be responsible and accountable for myself in ways that can be downright torturous. To see my ego and resentments for what they are and to understand how they contribute to the general disintegration of the systems in which I work is very humbling.

Ginny Cunningham—writer, wife, mother, and grandmother, Pittsburgh, Pennsylvania justice! But she will not succeed if she tries to solve all the problems of the hospital or the medical profession at once or even one problem completely. She must break those problems down into more manageable issues.

Part of that, quite frankly, will depend on how well she has organized and how powerful her organization is. If it is truly strong and united, with trained leadership and a mobilized constituency, she will be able to tackle bigger issues. Initially, she might have to start small. For example, if one of the problems is that people without health insurance are being turned away from the hospital, she might have to negotiate a policy that commits the hospital to admitting ten uninsured people a month. Having won this little victory, she has already made the hospital function just a little better, but she can also use the victory to build her organization and go on to bigger and better things.

Operating this way is difficult for some people. They consider this to be working for insignificant reforms while the larger problems remain. There may be some truth to this, but unless and until we build an organization powerful enough to overturn the system completely, it may be our only option. Part of the question may be how we view our relationship to God's power. If we think that only divine intervention can bring about social justice, then we can

A few years back, my wife, Kathy, was the director of a senior center operated by Catholic Charities. One of her unmarried clerical assistants found out that she was pregnant at the same time that Kathy's boss decided to cut the woman's hours, which would have made her a part-time employee and cut off her insurance benefits. This would have jeopardized the health of mother and child.

Kathy pleaded with her supervisor not to do this, but it was only when Kathy went over his head to the division manager that the secretary's hours—and her health insurance—were restored. Needless to say, the woman still has a positive image of the church because of Kathy's action.

Richard M. Stojak—diocesan family-life director, husband, father, and grandfather—about Kathleen K. Stojak, pastoral minister, wife, mother, and grandmother
Keller, Texas

pretty much sit back and wait for that to happen. If we believe that God works through us to make the world a better place, then we might have to be willing to take whatever baby steps we can, relying on God to keep us moving toward the perfect society, in which every problem will be solved.

Is working for social justice part of the spirituality of work? It is if it is part of a comprehensive approach to what it means

> **How do we** as a Christian community transform the way our collective work gets done so that we can better ensure a sustainable economy that does less harm to the ecology, develop ways for people to work in patterns that are creative and enabling of relationships, reduce overall work stress, and provide just sharing of goods and even work itself? The real challenge of the spirituality of work is to transform the deep structures of work and commerce itself.
>
> **Barbara J. Fleischer**—college educator
> New Orleans, Louisiana

to encounter God in our workplace. As with all the disciplines of the spirituality of work, working to make the system work should be judged by its results—in the life of the individual practicing it and in the workplace itself.

Practicing the Discipline

- Keep a list of the things that need to be changed about each of the institutions in which you live and work. On the opposite side of the paper, make another list of the things that these institutions do well and that you need to support and maintain. Call these your "If the World Were Perfect" lists. Add to them each time you notice something good or bad about the "systems" in which you operate.

- Pick one item from your "If the World Were Perfect" lists each year. Start or join an organization that can do something to either change or maintain that policy or procedure.

- Talk to someone in your workplace about social-justice matters at least once a week.

- Join or help form one organization that is trying to improve one of the systems in which you operate.

- Take a problem that you care about and try to think of ten issues— small things that you and your organization could win on that problem—that would make the system in which you operate a little better. Try to make progress on half of them in the next year.

Chapter 12

Engaging in Ongoing Personal and Professional Development

Now if thou compare deed to deed, there is difference
betwixt washing of dishes and preaching of the word of
God; but as touching to please God, none at all.

William Tyndale

The final discipline for consideration in this book (which, I remind my readers, is meant to be among the first—not the last—words on the spirituality of work) is also perhaps the most traditional. This discipline most closely fits the traditional understandings of what it means to be spiritual.

Most of us still regard spirituality as having to do with our interior life—the development of our souls, the building of our spiritual "character"—prior to or at least separate from our action (work) in the world. I once wrote an article titled "Let's Create a Spirituality of Work That Works" for *U.S. Catholic* magazine. The editors, who are very sympathetic to my point of view, sent out a questionnaire to their readers, asking for their response to various statements, including one I found very curious: "No one's spiritual life can flourish without occasional experiences of silence and solitude." An overwhelming number of the respondents agreed with the statement, which did not surprise me. Either the answer is obvious and universal (we all need peace and quiet sometimes) or the question implies that traditional forms of contemplation are absolutely necessary for everyone's spiritual life.

One respondent wrote, "Pierce's article still poses work and contemplation as things in opposition. Contemplation prepares us to work, and those we encounter in our work provide seeds for contemplation." Another said, "All the spirituality-of-work disciplines will come easily to those who use their private time to pray and meditate. Using 'gimmicks' may help; the true stresses of work can only be handled by those who are deeply rooted in their faith and who are able to incorporate that in their daily habits." A third respondent added, "While Pierce would probably characterize prayer as 'contemplative,' prayer allows God to shape our viewpoint on work so that the supposed discontinuity between work and the rest of our lives disappears."

So are the disciplines of a spirituality of work just "gimmicks"— poor cousins of the tried-and-true contemplative disciplines of prayer, reflection, and other spiritual exercises? Or can these workplace disciplines enable practitioners to attain a true spiritual state without practicing the contemplative disciplines?

The answer to this question lies, I believe, in the discipline of ongoing personal and professional development. It is in the context of preparing ourselves for work in every facet of our lives that the traditional spiritual disciplines fit into the spirituality of work. In other words, what is usually considered "spiritual activity" is actually a small portion of all those activities we undertake to prepare and sustain us for the world of work. Remember, we defined work as "all the effort (paid or unpaid) we exert to make the world a better place, a little closer to the way God would have things." The discipline of engaging in ongoing personal and professional development, then, includes anything that prepares us for work, including—but certainly not limited to—prayer and contemplation.

> **To add depth** to my work, I have treated myself to taking courses to obtain a certificate in holistic nursing. The first part of this program is self-caring. I am asked to commit myself to time for the exploration of my own body-mind-spirit. It also involves a structured practicum with such things as journaling on self-care and contemplative spirituality.
>
> It is the consistent rhythm of everyday practice that will help us see and live our work as a spiritual path, and I am struggling to make this happen. I find that the deadlines of this coursework offer me the structure I need. It opens me to God's speaking to me through my intuition about how I can help nurses and other caregivers see the spirituality of their work.
>
> **Julia Balzer Briley**—nurse, author, speaker, wife, and mother
> Cumming, Georgia

Professional Development

Is there a spirituality to keeping oneself current in one's occupational field? I once had a pastor who said, "I have not had time to read a book since the Second Vatican Council." This was in 1975, about ten years after the Council had ended, and it struck me how much change

I tape every sixth sermon I give and evaluate it a few weeks later. I have learned awful and wonderful things about my preaching that way.

Donna Schaper—United Church of Christ minister, writer, and mother, Miami, Florida

---

Ongoing personal and professional development is a spiritual discipline to the person who practices it, *if* he or she regards his or her work the same way. If work is drudgery, then personal and professional development is also drudgery. If work is merely earning bread by the sweat of one's brow, then personal and professional development is too. If work is a competitive game, then personal and professional development is done to gain a competitive advantage. Whatever work is for a person, that is what personal and professional development is.

David Neff—magazine editor, husband, father, and grandfather, Wheaton, Illinois

in thinking had taken place in that man's field in that time. He was, perhaps not coincidentally, a very poor pastor.

Some professions, such as medicine, require ongoing professional development just to stay certified to practice in particular fields or perform certain procedures. Other professions, such as teaching, reward but do not necessarily require ongoing professional development. Most occupations, however, have no mechanism for demanding or even encouraging practitioners to keep up-to-date on their knowledge or skills.

Many people do this on their own. They would not think of working in their chosen field without making sure they knew the latest thinking and techniques. Such professional development is costly and time-consuming, but when it is practiced regularly and with the right attitude, it can be a discipline of the spirituality of work.

We have all known people who—like my post–Vatican II pastor—were too busy or lazy or thoughtless or irresponsible to keep up their professional development. If that field is engineering or psychology or a similar work in which people's lives depend on the competency of the practitioner, the results can be tragic and public.

In other cases, incompetence caused by lack of ongoing professional development is merely irritating or embarrassing. Who wants a barber or hairdresser who doesn't know the latest style? Or to go to a restaurant where the chef or the waiters haven't been properly trained? But is such professional development spiritual? It is, by definition, if it gets the worker in touch with the deeper meaning and transcendent nature of his or her work.

For example, I know a social worker who subscribes to virtually every journal in her field. When I asked her why, she responded, "I just wouldn't feel that I was doing a good job for my clients if I didn't know the latest thinking. It makes me feel that I am doing everything I can to get myself ready for work. Then I can leave the rest to God."

Mental and Physical Health

Much like professional development, mental and physical health have obvious effects on our ability to do our best work. Also like professional development, health is something that is usually taken for granted. Few jobs require that employees work out physically or take care of their mental health. Yet who could deny that one's physical and mental health contribute to spiritual awareness in the workplace? If we are tired, sick, or depressed, how can we have the energy to notice the presence of God where we work?

So it is obvious that taking care of our physical and mental health can be a spiritual discipline. I have a simple example from my own life. When I am practicing this discipline, I try to take a short walk in a park near our house between 6:30 and 7:00 a.m. Whenever I do this regularly over a period of several weeks, I not only feel better, but I also find myself much more aware of the spiritual nature of my work. Unfortunately, as with all of the disciplines in this book, I often find myself falling out of this practice, and I can go weeks or even months without taking my walk. My body becomes much more sluggish, I am more susceptible to colds and other illnesses, and my spiritual life suffers.

Here is the key point of this experience in regards to spirituality. While I am walking, I do not pray or meditate. I could, and I have even tried to do so. I have found, however, that it is much more enjoyable and effective for me to listen to the radio. I don't listen to Christian or religious programming or even play a religious tape. Instead, I listen to music or news or sports. I do let my mind wander— over what is going on in the world or at work or with my family. I notice the beauty of nature, the other people in the park, and the exhilaration I get from the physical activity. Many times, although clearly not always or even often, my thoughts will turn to "spiritual" matters—the meaning of life, what God is really like, how I could be a better person, or what I could do to help make the world a better place.

Whether my thoughts are "spiritual" or not, however, the experience certainly is. When I take my daily walk on a disciplined basis, I am always more spiritually aware during the day. I attribute this to the discipline of walking itself, not to any piety I might practice while I am doing it.

Mental health operates the same way. If we take care of our minds—with plenty of rest, hobbies, reading, vacations, and other leisure activities—then this will be reflected in our spiritual lives. These practices do not have to be overlaid with religious content to be spiritually effective.

Ongoing Education

Different from, but related to, professional development is the discipline of engaging in ongoing, lifelong education. Such education may not be related to one's occupation or have any overtly spiritual content to contribute to the spirituality of our work. Few would argue that finishing high school or obtaining a college degree or degrees does not contribute to competency in our work. There are certain skills that are necessary for virtually every occupation. But beyond the obvious need for education that relates to our profession, isn't there spiritual value

I spend half an hour each morning in centering prayer or quiet meditation. In addition to the beauty of that time, there's a place within me where I can return during my hectic workday to reconnect with the presence I experienced that morning. A mantra I use during prayer is "Be here now," and I repeat it often during the day as well.

I pray for particular people in my workplace at a separate time before going to work. I have two categories: those I really like and those who are difficult for me to work with. I also turn over to the Spirit particular projects on which I am working.

Once I get to my office, I read a few pages of something inspirational for my work. Before I pick up my voice mails, I try to remember (but don't always succeed) to listen to God first. I sometimes say, "Speak, Lord, I am listening."

The challenge for me is to be fully effective in my work while remaining aware that the workplace is sacred space filled with holy people, all held in the context of a power much greater than ourselves. In an attempt to gather with others who are on a similar path, I have started a special-interest group we call "Spirit in the Workplace." This is not a firm-sponsored initiative but rather several of us who gather on our own time. Topics we have dialogued about include: spirit in the workplace, balance in life, core values and how they impact our performance, trust, and competition versus collaboration. We've met monthly for over a year now, and last month I brought in an outside speaker whose topic was "Bringing your whole self to work."

Mary Jo Hazard—corporate trainer, wife, and mother, Naperville, Illinois in learning for its own sake? Don't we, in fact, become better work-ers—or at least better people to work with—if we know more about the world around us?

This is, of course, the basic argument for a liberal arts education. One of the most troubling developments in current education is the specialization that is taking place earlier and earlier in college and even in high school. "I don't need to study history or English literature because I'm going to be a computer programmer" seems to be the argument. And this idea is too often accepted, if not promoted, by educational institutions. This trend is driven in part by the sheer amount of information that is needed if a person is to succeed in so many professions today. But the specialization of education also seems to be driven by the market. We are educated for a job, not for life.

Having a job is a very good thing; just ask people who don't have one. But do we really want lawyers who don't appreciate Shakespeare or janitors who don't know history or business people who aren't fascinated by theology? The answer to this dilemma is the discipline of ongoing education.

Reading is a good place to start. Let's say we were to read twelve books a year that have on their surface absolutely nothing to do with our work. Novels, biographies, current events, sports, travel—it doesn't matter what the topic, it is the discipline that is important. Would this make us better workers? Might we be more

> I try to start each morning by reading a few lines from the Bible. Since I write for a living, I am reading from a King James version for its lovely language. I was emboldened to do so, despite exegetical problems with that transla-tion, when I read of an accomplished features writer who did the same. She may have been a deeply devout per-son, but she explained the habit largely in terms of liking the language of the King James. Maybe that made it more palatable to her secular colleagues as well.
>
> **Christopher D. Ringwald**—writer, teacher, husband, and father, Albany, New York

content, more open to noticing new ideas and opportunities, simply more interesting to be around? This discipline might even be incorporated into our workdays. We could read (or listen to audio books) on our commute or during lunch or work breaks. Some people even organize book discussion groups in their workplace. This not only accomplishes the discipline of ongoing education but also builds support and community in the workplace.

> **I've been trying** to be aware and awake for many years. Every day I begin again to be open to mindfulness. I need my own morning stretch of quiet prayer time in order to be more fully awake to the divine presence throughout the rest of my day. I am a high introvert, so I don't know if this need for "going apart" is as true for extroverts.
>
> **Joyce Rupp, OSM**—author and retreat facilitator, member of a religious community Des Moines, Iowa

Once we've got the idea of ongoing education as a spiritual discipline, many other options present themselves. We can take adult education courses at a school or through correspondence, surf the Internet for something other than shopping, watch educational television once a week or once a day, attend a religious education series at our church, even pursue an advanced degree late in life.

Interaction with Colleagues

For the past dozen years, I have met with a group of Chicago-area businesspeople about once a month to discuss the practical problems of being a Christian business manager. We have discussed such issues as terminations and layoffs; stewardship of our businesses; balancing work, personal, and family life (both for ourselves and our employees); and paying a just wage in a market economy. To tell the truth, it is a pain for me to get to most of the meetings. My business is not in downtown Chicago, where the meetings are held, and most of the sessions are either very early in the morning or at lunchtime. Still, I make most meetings. It is a spiritual discipline, and I do it because it raises my awareness of the spirituality of my own work.

Part of the discipline of ongoing personal and professional development is to find or organize a group of people with whom you can share your spiritual journey on a more explicit and profound level. This can be done and is being done in a variety of ways. Some parishes have formed "small Christian communities"—subsets of the larger congregation—that meet regularly to share and discuss their faith in their daily lives. Often work is one of the regular topics, and sometimes the groups are even organized by occupation. Usually these meetings are held in homes or parish facilities, and the groups are meant to be ongoing.

There are also many groups that meet regularly in the workplace itself. Many of them are explicitly religious, such as prayer breakfasts or Bible-study and faith-sharing groups. For those who are so inclined, these can be an excellent spiritual practice. For many who, like me, are uncomfortable with displays of piety—especially in the workplace—we can still participate in groups that get at the meaning of work and life without forcing the issue. A book-of-the-month discussion group might accomplish this. Several dioceses now sponsor "First Fridays" and other lecture series in downtown locations. It might be as simple a matter as finding one or two

Without some interior prayer that touches some depth of soul, we will continue to hunger. We will try to feed that hunger with "good works," but the works in the marketplace will be like the kind of social work that causes us to burn out, no matter what our intentions when we begin.

We must enter the "interior darkness" through prayer or else carry an emptiness with us into the world. The spiritual hunger proper to all humans cannot be fed with success, money, control, power, or whatever other drug we might use.

People of prayer attract others in the workplace because they are a channel of the Spirit. Those without some deep prayer life simply promote various programs and projects. I am too often in the latter situation—trudging along, gnashing my teeth.

Terry Ryan, CSP—Catholic priest and pastor, member of a religious community Knoxville, Tennessee

One thing I have learned over the years is that I cannot serve others, including my family and those I serve through my job, if I have overextended myself and take no time to "refill my well." It is when I have given too much of myself away that I lose all perspective on how to maintain or return to balance in my life.

In the last year I have experienced the death of my father, the return and metastasis of breast cancer in my mother, and a new diagnosis of breast cancer in my sister. I tried to continue to do my job as effectively as always while being available to support my family through these and other crises that came up. But I knew that this was taking its toll as my energy and enthusiasm for my work declined. I discussed with my family, my spiritual director, and my employer my need for a week of silent retreat. In the past, I could never have considered this as I would have felt guilty for taking this time (and the money) from my family, but they were all very understanding. Through thinking in new ways, I was able to create a directed retreat for myself at a beach in Florida (when there were few tourists) for less than the cost of a simple directed retreat here in Minnesota. My employer paid the airfare out of our development budget.

I was in Florida, and my director was in Minnesota. I called her for prearranged telephone appointments. The experience not only filled my well but set a new model for employee development at our organization. I learned more from my silent directed retreat week at the beach (on vacation with God, as my spiritual director suggested) than I have in several spirituality-and-work conferences that I have attended. Since much of my work involves helping others learn to find balance in their lives and work, my supervisor had no trouble justifying that I needed to find balance in my own life to teach it.

Wouldn't it be wonderful if all employers could appreciate the renewed creativity and zest for work that comes from taking retreat or "Sabbath" time?

Lisa Murray—spiritual director and program coordinator, wife, and mother
Eagan, Minnesota

"kindred souls" in your workplace and discussing things with them on a deeper level on a regular basis—over lunch once a week or daily at the watercooler for five minutes.

The point of this discipline is that we cannot practice spirituality totally on our own. We need others to both support and challenge us, including our colleagues in the workplace.

Other Spiritualities

One of the most successful and intriguing books on the spirituality of work is Lewis Richmond's *Work as a Spiritual Practice*. It is marketed as "a guide to developing and maintaining a spiritual life on the job, drawn from the teachings and practices of Buddhist tradition." What is interesting is the parallel between Richmond's Buddhist practices and traditional Christian spirituality. Both stress the development of the soul as the goal of spirituality. "A spiritual practice," Richmond says, "is not a warm-up or a rehearsal but an end in itself, an activity that expresses and develops our inner life."

One practice that helps my ongoing personal and professional development is meeting regularly with people outside my immediate work. For example, I meet with my pastor once a week. I am the chair of our church council, so it works for both of us, but our discussions are more wide-ranging than just church business. We look at spiritual transformation, stewardship as a way of life, and other topics that relate directly to my work. I meet with a friend once a quarter who owns his own company and is a very disciplined thinker on values, continuous improvement of both product and personnel, and other work-related subjects. He is a very thought-provoking person. I also meet every couple of months with my former boss. He is a very spiritual person—the son of a pastor and very active in his church. He is way ahead of me theologically and spiritually.

Another practice I have is to listen to my employees, to go to their meetings, to observe how they deal with the communities they serve. I learn a lot about what is important to people, what their passions are. I always find that I learn a lot about myself as well. It provides grist for my personal reflection and learning.

Mark Linder—municipal department director and husband
Santa Cruz, California

The best of both the Buddhist and the Christian contemplative traditions view their spiritual disciplines as preparation for going out into the world of action, including the workplace. Richmond claims that among some schools of Buddhism, monks were expected to leave the monastery after their formal training was concluded and were only qualified to teach after years of travel and life experience. "Monks who had grown too attached to the monastic life were sometimes described as 'demons of the dark cave,'" Richmond reports. Similar warnings against withdrawal from the world can be found throughout Christian spiritual teachings.

I do not consider either traditional Christian spiritualities or the spiritual practices of other world religions to be antithetical to or even competitive with the practical spiritual disciplines we can apply to our work. Many people find that practicing "centering prayer" or praying "mantras" or reading the Hebrew Scriptures or the Koran daily make them better, or at least more spiritually aware, people in the workplace. I have good friends who swear by the Ignatian spiritual exercises, who find a visit to a Trappist monastery just the thing they need, who are practitioners of Franciscan or Dominican or Salesian or Benedictine or many other Christian "spiritualities." All of these people assure me that the disciplines they follow are designed to send them out into the workplace better equipped to discover God there.

I have not the slightest doubt that these people are telling the truth. I know this not only by their testimony but by their actions. Many of them are among the holiest practitioners of the spirituality of work I have encountered. If we are going to be the most spiritual workers we can be, then we will follow every path that improves our awareness of the presence of God in our work.

Practicing the Discipline

- Subscribe to a journal or periodical in your field.

- Go to at least one professional development course or seminar every year.

- Exercise at least twenty minutes every day, at least five days a week, at the same time each day.

- Take a "mental-health day" once every few months—as a vacation, personal, or sick day, if necessary.

- Read a book each month that has nothing to do with your work. Organize or join a book-of-the-month discussion group, either at work or in your community.

- Join or organize some kind of small faith-sharing group. If this is not possible, find one or two people you can go to lunch with monthly to discuss the deeper meaning of your work.

- Investigate a traditional spirituality—Christian, Jewish, Buddhist, Muslim, Hindu, or any other. See how it might apply to your work life. Practice it for a year and then judge whether to continue or try another.

An Invitation

Is there a spirituality of work? Can God really be found in the hustle and bustle of daily life as easily (or as fully) as in silence, solitude, and simplicity? Even after working on this book for a couple of years, I can't fully answer that question.

It is pretty clear to me that God is present in our workplaces. There is too much experience, too much testimony, and too many examples of people experiencing the divine presence in their work to deny or even doubt it. As Pierre Teilhard de Chardin put it in *Hymn of the Universe,* "[God] is, in a sense, at the point of my pen, my pick, my paintbrush, my needle—and my heart and my thought. It is by carrying to completion the stroke, the line, the stitch I am working on that I shall lay hold on the ultimate end towards which my will at its deepest levels tends."

Yet the workplace is a difficult place in which to "be spiritual." It is noisy, crowded, complex, competitive, materialistic, tiring, frustrating, dangerous, busy, secular. To find God there, we have to work (there's that word again) hard at it, and most of our traditional spiritual disciplines are not well designed to help us do that. That is why I have tried to outline this idea of developing a new set of disciplines that might help me and others practice the spirituality of work. I believe that these and other disciplines can be practiced by anyone— even the busiest or the least pious amongst us—in our workplace. Like all spiritual disciplines, however, they would have to be done conscientiously, faithfully, and regularly. If they are to be judged authentic, they must change our awareness of the presence of God and of the ultimate meaning of our work as well as impact how our work is done and what results our work produces.

Are the disciplines I have named the right ones? Are they stated correctly? Are they too secular or mundane? Are there other, better disciplines of the spirituality of work? I don't know the answers to those questions, but I am mightily interested in them. That is why I have written this book and am committed to continuing this discussion with like-minded people of all occupations and faiths. I invite any of the readers of this book to contact me, either through the publisher or directly by e-mail at spiritualitywork@aol.com. I promise, as one of my own spiritual disciplines, to send you a few paragraphs on the spirituality of work about once a month. I will invite your responses and share them as much as possible with others, just as I have tried to do in this book.

Is this worth the effort? I believe it is, for if we cannot develop a functioning spirituality of work, then both our work and our spirituality are impoverished. I'd like to end with my favorite quote on the spirituality of work, even if it does not mention the divinity. It is from poet David Whyte's *Crossing the Unknown Sea: Work as Pilgrimage of Identity*.

> Work leaves its mark on each of us. Our growing characters and memories are formed by the first images graven by work on our growing sense of the world. The cast of our mother's face as she mentions the office, the smolder in our father's eye as he speaks of his boss. Toddlers see their mother leave happily or wearily in the morning, seven-year-olds watch their father's face as he enters the door at night. Teenagers become helpless before their parents' unemployment or just as angry if they work too much. Inside each of us is layer after layer of accumulated experience and memory slowly constellating itself into our adult universe of work.
>
> Wherever we work, we need courage both to remember what we are about and, according to the tenor of our times, reimagine ourselves while we are doing it. We are not alone in this endeavor but secretly joined to all those who struggle out loud where we have not yet begun to speak, or when we are loud and vociferous, to those who labor painfully and secretly beside us. We are joined especially with those now silent who have come before us. We represent not only ourselves but those who have gifted us the possibilities of the present. In the satisfaction

of good work is not only the fulfillment of a very personal dream but the harvest of generations of hope and toil.

If work can be all that, then, "bidden or not bidden," how can God not be present?

Sources

All quotations (other than the epigraphs that begin each chapter, which are not referenced) are from "Faith and Work in Cyberspace," a free discussion group that I maintain online, unless noted below.

Quote from John Shea (p. 3) is from a private conversation.

Quote from Eugene Kennedy (p. 3) is from a Religious News Service article reprinted in *The Catholic New World,* August 30–September 6, 1998.

Quotes from Mike Royko and Abraham Lincoln (p. 3–4) are from *Heigh-Ho! Heigh-Ho!: Funny, Insightful, Encouraging, and Sometimes Painful Quotes about Work* by Terry Sullivan and Al Gini (Chicago: ACTA Publications, 1994), pp. 98, 115.

Reference (p. 5) is to *Christian Spirituality: The Essential Guide to the Most Influential Spiritual Writings of the Christian Tradition,* edited by Frank N. Magill and Ian P. McGreal (San Francisco: Harper & Row, 1988).

Quotes from Richard Foster (p. 7) are from *A Celebration of Discipline: The Path to Spiritual Growth* (San Francisco: Harper & Row, 1988), p. 15.

Quote from Parker Palmer (p. 8) is from *The Active Life: A Spirituality of Work, Creativity, and Caring* (San Francisco: Harper & Row, 1990), p. 2.

The stories "The Fasting Monk" (p. 9) and "God's Fruit Stand" (p. 42) are told by John Shea in his book *The Legend of the Bells and Other*

Tales: Stories of the Human Spirit (Chicago: ACTA Publications, 1996), pp. 29, 39.

Quotes from Thomas à Kempis (p. 11) are from *The Imitation of Christ,* edited by Paul M. Bechtel (Chicago: Moody Press, 1980), pp. 24, 60, 69.

Quotes from Paul Wilkes (pp. 13, 16) are from *Beyond the Walls: Monastic Wisdom for Everyday Life* (New York: Doubleday, 1999), pp. xxi, 238.

Quote from Mary Southard (p. 13) is from a private conversation.

Quote from Brother Lawrence (pp. 15–16) is from *The Practice of the Presence of God: Updated in Today's Language* by Ellyn Sanna (Uhrichsville, Ohio: Barbour Publishing, 1998), pp. 21, 24.

Quote from James Behrens (p. 16) is from *Grace Is Everywhere: Reflections of an Aspiring Monk* (Chicago: ACTA Publications, 1999), p. 141.

Quote from Lily Tomlin (p. 16) is from *Heigh-Ho! Heigh-Ho!: Funny, Insightful, Encouraging, and Sometimes Painful Quotes about Work* by Terry Sullivan and Al Gini (Chicago: ACTA Publications, 1994), p. 115.

Quotes from Mary Beth Sammons and Michael Coffield (pp. 32–33) are from Ms. Sammons's article "Sacred Spaces and Desktop Devotions," which appeared in *The Catholic New World,* February 13, 1998.

Quote from Peg Streep (p. 33) is from *Altars Made Easy: A Complete Guide to Creating Your Own Sacred Space* (HarperSanFrancisco, 1997), p. 33.

Quotes from William Burke (p. 44) are from *Protect Us from All Anxiety: Meditations for the Depressed* (Chicago: ACTA Publications, 1998), pp. 27–28.

Story by Paul Wilkes (p. 50) is from a private conversation.

Story of Allen-Edmonds shoe factory (pp. 91–92) is by William Droel from *Confident & Competent: A Challenge for the Lay Church* (Notre Dame, IN: Ave Maria Press, 1987), p. 37.

Quote from D. H. Lawrence (p. 99) is from his poem "Wages," as found in *The Oxford Book of Work,* edited by Keith Thomas (Oxford; New York: Oxford University Press, 1999), p. 35.

Quote from Ron Kreitmeyer (p. 126) is from his article "What Social Justice Is—and Is Not," which appeared in *The Catholic Spirit,* February 12, 1998.

Quote from U. S. Catholic bishops (p. 127–128) is from their statement "Lay Discipleship for Justice in the Millennium," approved at their annual 1998 meeting.

Quote from Bill Droel (p. 129) is from a private conversation .

Quotes (p. 136) are from unpublished responses to a questionnaire sent to readers by the editors of *U.S. Catholic* magazine requesting feedback on an article by Gregory F. Augustine Pierce titled "Let's Create a Spirituality of Work That Works," which was published in the magazine's September 1999 issue.

Quotes from Lewis Richmond (pp. 146–147) are from *Work as a Spiritual Practice: A Practical Buddhist Approach to Inner Growth and Satisfaction on the Job* (New York: Broadway Books, 1999), pp. 13, 26.

Quote from Pierre Teilhard de Chardin (p. 149) is from *Hymn of the Universe,* translated by Simon Bartholomew (New York: Harper & Row, 1965), p. 84.

Quote from David Whyte (pp. 150–151) is from *Crossing the Unknown Sea: Work as a Pilgrimage of Identity,* as it appeared in his "Letter from the House," winter 1999–2000.

Acknowledgments

I'd like to thank the following people:

Bill Droel, my best friend and the person who has taught me the most about the spirituality of work. Also, Russ Barta, and Ed Marciniak, may they rest in peace, and all the other leaders of the National Center for the Laity, who have kept the light focused on the idea that the primary vocation of the laity is in and to the world.

Joe Sullivan, Paul Fullmer, Bill Yacullo, and all the members of Business Executives for Economic Justice, who have showed me that business is a vocation.

Ed Chambers, Msgr. John Egan, and all the organizers and leaders of the Industrial Areas Foundation, who have demonstrated what social justice is and how to do it.

Fr. Gerry Weber, Mary Buckley, Tom Artz, John Dewan, and all my colleagues at ACTA Publications and the Catholic Book Publishers Association, who have given me an opportunity to do work that is fulfilling and proved to me that the workplace can, indeed, be a holy place.

LaVonne Neff, Vinita Wright, Rebecca Johnson, Fr. George Lane, Leslie Waters, Erin VanWerden, and the entire staff of Loyola Press, who encouraged me to write this book, edited it superbly, and produced it with grace.

My parents, Fran and Mary Pierce, and my seven siblings, who formed me from a very early age in the spirituality of work, and my wife, Kathy, and our three children, Abby, Nate, and Zack, who supported my writing of this book—even during our vacation to Disney World!

Finally, the participants in "Faith and Work in Cyberspace," who have dialogued with me on this subject for many years and whose insights have helped shape my thinking in many ways. Many of their comments are sprinkled throughout this book.